Liz Parry's
SPANISH
PHRASE
BOOK

All the words and phrases
you need in everyday
situations – together with
an insight into Spanish
customs

SANTANA BOOKS

First published in 2004

Copyright © Prensa Malagueña.
The Author asserts the moral right to be
identified as the author of this work.

Designed by Chris Fajardo
Illustrations by Elgar

Liz Parry's Spanish Phrase Book
is published by Ediciones Santana S.L.,
Apartado 422, Fuengirola 29640 (Malaga) Spain.
Tel. 952 485 838. Fax 952 485 367.
E-mail info@santanabooks.com
www.santanabooks.com

Printed in Spain by Gráficas San Pancracio S.l.

Depósito Legal: MA-905/2004

ISBN: 84-89954-37-2

While I was writing this book, I often had two readers in mind – a couple who learned Spanish so that they could get more out of their visits to Spain by talking to its people. They have read it all, inspired parts of it, and make an appearance in some of its pages.

This book is for my parents, with much love and many thanks.

About the author

Liz Parry was born in Salisbury, not far from Stonehenge, and grew up in Warlingham (Surrey) and Retford (North Nottinghamshire). After studying Spanish in Granada, she lived in Birmingham and Oxford before moving permanently back to Spain with her Spanish husband. When asked how long she has lived in this country, she will just say "more than half my life!"

After several jobs, including simultaneous interpreting at a summer sports university ("bad for the brain but good for weight loss") and taking out time to have children, she started working for Malaga's weekly newspaper *SUR in English* and is now the editor. Her book is based on the weekly column she writes about Spain, its customs and its language.

CONTENTS

ODDS AND ENDS

INTRODUCTION

In my job as editor of Malaga's *"SUR In English"* weekly newspaper, I constantly hear readers express the wish to learn Spanish and communicate with their Spanish neighours and local trades people. Some will try to pick up the language by just listening and talking, which can be a relative painless but rather slow process.

Others will get stuck into a grammar book or take lessons. There are countless language schools along the *Costas*. It goes without saying the results are worth the effort. We all know – because we are told over and over again – that learning Spanish enriches our lives in Spain. Even so, few of us are going to make the effort and become fluent Spanish speakers, but instead will content ourselves with gathering enough key words and phrases to get by.

If you are one of these people, this book is for you. It will not lead you into the minefield of Spanish grammar, putting you through the torture of countless conjugations of verbs and the dreaded Subjunctive, but instead will provide you with some easy-to-learn words and phrases that will help you to handle situations that you as a foreign resident in Spain find yourself in all the time.

But there is one important thing to remember. You won't get far knowing some key Spanish words and phrases if you don't pronounce them correctly. Here, believe it or not, you have an advantage over the Spanish student, who is totally baffled by English pronunciation and will never fully understand why Bough, Through, Though and Cough don't rhyme with Enough.

Unlike English, Spanish is phonetic, which means the sounds of letters, with very rare exceptions, are always the same. Once you've learned the right sound for each letter, you should be able to pronounce the language correctly. Just remember to put the stress on the penultimate syllable. Any exception to this rule is indicated by an accent.

The pronunciation of some Spanish letters is the same as in English. These are b, f, k, l, n, p, s and t. The rest are pronounced as follows:

a – as in fat.

c – a hard "c" as in "cat", except when it comes before an "e" or an "i", when it is pronounced like the "th" in thin.

ch – considered as one letter, as the "ch" in "church".

d – a hard "d" as in "dog" at the beginning of a word and after "n" or "l"; as the "th" in thin between vowels and at the end of a word.

g – a hard "g" as in "go". Before an "e" or an "i", it sounds a bit like a Scot pronouncing the "ch" in "loch". Ask a Scot to have a go at it, or persuade a Spanish acquaintance to say *"gente"* (people) or *"cogí"* (I took). This type of "g" is often softened in southern Spain to not much more than an English "h". In *"gui"* and *"gue"*, the "u" is silent and serves to harden the "g", as in *"guía"* (guide).

h – is always silent. "Hotel" is pronounced "otel" and *"hora"* is pronounced *"ora"*.

i – is short, as in "fit".

j – like the "ch" in "loch", the same as "g" before "e" or "i".

ll – considered a separate letter and pronounced *"el-ye"*. When placed in a word, the second "l" serves as a consonant before the following vowel, as in *"paella"*, pronounced *"pie-el-ya"*.

o – a short "o" as in top.

q – always followed by a silent "u" and pronounced like an English "k", as in "key".

r – pronounced with a slight roll between the vowels and a stronger roll after the consonant and at the beginning of a sentence.

rr – considered a separate letter and pronounced with a strong roll. Try practicing with the tongue-twister *"El perro de San Ramón no tiene rabo"* (St. Raymond's dog has no tail).

u – as in shoe.

v – usually pronounced like a "b", but often sounds like a cross between a "b" and a "v" in the middle of words.

w – not native to the Spanish language and only found in words of foreign origin.

x – as in expert.

y – as in "yes" when preceding a vowel, and sounding like the "ee" in "seen" (though a bit shorter) at the end of a word or standing alone as a conjunction.

z – pronounced like the "th" in "think".

Having learned how to pronounce your armful of Spanish words and phrases correctly, the next – and possibly hardest – step is to use them. Don't hold back. And remember, Spaniards will never laugh at your mistakes. On the contrary, they will think more of you for trying to speak their language, however much you mangle it.

SOCIALISING

Dinner Party

So your Spanish neighbours have invited you for dinner or you have taken the plunge and asked them round to your place for a meal. Either way, don't forget that Spaniards eat late. They won't want you to show up before nine, and conversely it would be a problem for them to arrive at your house before that time as they probably work until around eight.

You can turn up with a bottle of wine or some chocolates or flowers. If you know them quite well, you can even offer to bring the dessert. Whoever provides the dessert, the hosts or guests, it's quite acceptable to buy it at a shop, though the Spaniards I know would appreciate your baking something as they think Brits excel in making puddings and cakes.

Pondering the subject of dining etiquette, I visited the BBC's website and on its International Dining Etiquette page I found a paragraph on Spain which said: "In a *tapas* bar in Spain, all the detritus – pips, crumbs, disposable napkins, cigarette butts, etc – are thrown on the floor." You can be sure this does not happen in a Spanish home!

Os invito a comer/cenar el viernes – Would you like to come for lunch/dinner on Friday?

Los niños también, por supuesto – And the children, of course

Haremos una barbacoa – We'll have a barbecue

¿A qué hora debemos llegar? – What time should we arrive?

Sobre las nueve, ¿te parece? – About nine, does that sound OK?

Nosotros llevamos el postre – We'll provide dessert

Haré una tarta de chocolate – I'll make a chocolate cake

Te presento a mi prima Carmen – Let me introduce my cousin Carmen

Y su marido, Pepe – And her husband Pepe

Carmen me ha ayudado con la ensalada – Carmen helped me with the salad

Siéntate aquí a mi lado – You sit here, next to me

Así podemos hablar de nuestras cosas – That way we can have a nice talk (about "our things")

¡Qué bien huele! – Something smells good!

¿Me pasas la sal? – Would you pass the salt?

Toma un poquito más – Have a bit more

No puedo, de verdad – I really couldn't

¡Qué rico! ¿Me das la receta? – This is delicious! Can I have the recipe?

Es una receta de mi abuela – It's my grandmother's recipe

Vamos a abrir otra botella – Let's open another bottle

El vino tiene que respirar – The wine needs to breathe

Visitors

Those of us who have taken up residence in Spain find that we have more friends and relatives than we remembered. Visits from the folk back home can be pleasant of course, but at times they can also be stressful. I can offer a few tips, learned from years of experience.

Always call the airport to find out if the plane is arriving on time, and allow a good half hour, even longer in summer, for them to claim their luggage and appear in the arrival hall. Tell them to go to the nearest bar, where you will be waiting in comfort instead of trying to make yourself visible in the crowd behind the travel representatives.

When you and your houseguests have caught up on all the news, you could start extolling all the wonderful places to see in your area and suggest they take a little trip in their hired car, and perhaps stay over a night or two in one of those charming rural hotels.

So far so good, but what happens when your houseguests from abroad meet your Spanish friends and neighbours or you take them on an excursion or to a Spanish event? You are instantly reduced from being the charming host or hostess to being a frazzled full-time translator. Just don't let anyone start telling jokes.

Vamos al aeropuerto a recoger a unos amigos – We are going to the airport to fetch some friends

Necesitaremos dos coches – We will need two cars

¿Información internacional? – The international information desk?

¿Me puede decir si el vuelo... llega a su hora? – Is flight number... arriving on time?

Estima su llegada a las dos de la madrugada – It is expected to land at two in the morning

Son cinco horas de demora – That's a five hour delay

Estamos esperando a unos amigos que llegan de ... We are waiting for some friends to arrive from...

Llegarán muy cansados – They'll be very tired

Te presento a mi amiga Beryl. Y sus hijos... Let me introduce my friend Beryl. And her children...

Es amiga de toda la vida – She's a friend from way back.

Fuimos al colegio juntas – We went to school together

Ha venido a pasar el mes de julio – She's come to spend the month of July

Y en agosto vienen mi primo y toda su familia – And in August my cousin is coming with all his family

Greetings

If you are going to get to know your Spanish neighbours and be introduced to their friends and relatives, you will have to get accustomed to their more exuberant way of greeting each other. Not for them a cool handshake and a murmured "How do you do?" – except on the most formal occasions.

When meeting for the first time, women usually kiss each other on both cheeks and men will do the same with women but will shake hands with other men. This is accompanied by the Spanish version of the "How do you do?" routine, in which one person says *"encantado"* (*"encantada"* if it is a woman speaking), which literally means "delighted", and the other says *"encantado"* or *"encantada"* back. If this seems a bit repetitive, you can opt for *"mucho gusto"* (a great pleasure) or *"igualmente"* (likewise).

At subsequent meetings you repeat the kissing or handshaking routine but substitute *"Hola, ¿cómo estás?"* (Hello, how are you?) or, if you haven't seen the other person for quite a time, *"Me alegro de verte"* (I'm happy to see you), to which *"Igualmente"* is a useful answer again.

You can add a third kiss to the regulation two when greeting a close female friend, and close male friends can indulge in a bit of back-slapping while shaking hands. Spanish men even hug and kiss their close male friends and relatives.

If in doubt, hang back just long enough to see what the other person intends to do and then join in, preferably with the same degree of enthusiasm.

A word about those tricky little Spanish words *Ud. (usted)* and *tu*, that can cause a lot of trouble. They are the equivalent of the French *vous* and *tu*, the former being the formal "you" and the latter being the more intimate form. Speaking to a relative, friend, someone your own age or a child, you would use *tu*, while older people, professional superiors and most strangers are addressed as *usted*.

These days, though, it would not be a disaster if you used the informal *tu* when you should use the formal *usted*, especially if you are a foreigner. I remember when I was presented to my future Spanish in-laws, who live in a small town where everyone knows everyone else, and my visit was a major event.

I started out well enough, kissing the women, addressing my elders as *usted* and so forth, but when we left and the whole town turned out to see us off, I was so overwhelmed and flustered, I remember being extremely formal with my future sister-in-law and kissing any number of men I'd never seen before. But nobody seem to mind.

Buenos días – Good morning

Buenas tardes – Good afternoon/evening

Buenas noches – Goodnight (also for greeting someone late at night)

Hola – Hello, hi

Adiós – Goodbye (Spaniards say *"Adiós"* to acquaintances, they pass in the street)

Hasta luego – See you later

Hasta ahora – See you soon

Hasta la vista – See you

Hasta mañana – See you tomorrow

¿Cómo estás? – How are you? (informal, to a friend)

¿Cómo está Vd? – How are you? (formal)

(Muy) bien, gracias – (Very) well, thank you

¿Qué tal? – How are you? How are things?

¿Qué hay? – How are you? What's new?

Making friends

When meeting a Spaniard for the first time, the first question you usually ask is "Where are you from?" – after which you most probably comment on the weather (*"¿Qué calor!"* or *"¡Qué frío!"* are useful phrases here). Then, if you both speak a little of the other's language, you find out whether you are going to be more comfortable conversing in Spanish or English.

Once you are over these hurdles, the next thing, at least according to many language books, is to find out where the other person comes from and what he or she does for a living. I suspect, though, that this is merely a device on the part of language teachers to get their pupils to use the verb "to be".

¿Hablas inglés? – Do you speak English?

¿Hablas mi idioma? – Do you speak my language?

¿De dónde eres? – Where are you from (informal)?

¿De dónde es? – Where are you from (formal)?

Soy inglés/a – I am English

Soy de Londres/del norte de Inglaterra – I am from London/the north of Ingland

Ellos son de Gales/Escocia – They are from Wales/Scotland

El es de Estados Unidos – He is from the USA

Mis amigos son suizos/alemanes/suecos/ daneses – My friends are Swiss/German/Swedish/ Danish

¿Qué haces? – What do you do?

¿Cómo se gana la vida? – How does he/she earn a living?

Tengo negocio – I have a business

¿Qué tipo de negocio? – What sort of business?

Soy jubilado/a – I am retired

Vivo de las rentas – I live off my private income

Estoy buscando trabajo – I am looking for work

Hay mucho trabajo en la construcción – There is a lot of work in the building sector

Y en el sector inmobiliario – And in the real estate sector

Es camarero/a, periodista, vendedor/a – He/she is a waiter/waitress, journalist, salesperson

Tiene suerte, tiene un trabajo fijo – He/she is lucky, he/she has a permanent job

Trabajo en una agencia, por horas – I work in an agency, by the hour

¿Tienes contrato y seguridad social? – Do you have a contract and social security?

Tengo un fijo más comisiones – I have a basic salary plus commission

Es pluriempleado/a – He/she has more than one job

Y los niños están en la guardería – And the children go to nursery school

What do you think? It doesn't look like
a cultural event to me

The dating game

I remember my Spanish mother-in-law telling her grand-children about her courting days, when she had to be home by 9pm, even if the film finished fifteen minutes later – and, when she and her *novio* played *ludo* in her house, how her grandmother, acting as chaperon, would wear sunglasses so that they wouldn't know if she was still watching them or had fallen asleep.

Her grandchildren were spellbound. They could hardly believe how much times have changed since those long-gone days of duennas and closely guarded young virgins. Young Spaniards today have more freedom than their grandparents ever dreamed of.

In a recent report on sex and Spanish youngsters, it was reported that out of six million people in Spain aged between fifteen and twenty four, more than a million have had unprotected sex, which means that 23.6 per cent of the boys and 23.1 per cent of the girls have run the risk of starting an unwanted pregnancy.

Even so, my daughter thinks Spanish youngsters are still less independent and not so sexually experienced as their British counterparts, and that this is due more to social factors than to different moral standards.

She says "British youngsters tend to leave the family home at an earlier age and therefore have a place to take a girlfriend to and be alone. Their Spanish couterparts would probably behave more openly if they had their own homes to take their partners to and if they didn't have their conservative, Catholic parents breathing down their necks."

Despite all these social changes, some of the old customs linger on, such as the *petición de mano* when the two families get together and the young man formally asks his *novia*'s father for her hand in marriage. And the pre-wedding visit to the couple's future home to inspect all the fittings and furnishings, right down to the hand-embroidered bed linen.

I was invited to one of these inspections and remember being shown some drawers full of "his" and "her" socks. This little ceremony is usually followed by a post-honeymoon invitation to the new home to see the wedding photographs.

Un ligue – A very casual relationship

Un rollo – Some you might enjoy snogging with, but that's about it

Un noviazgo – A serious relationship that could end in marriage.

Novio/novia – Boyfriend/girlfriend

Prometido/prometida – Fiancé/fiancée

Quieres salir a cenar conmigo? – Would you like to come out for dinner with me?

¿Tienes novio? – Have you got a boyfriend?

Salgo mucho con Juan, pero es sólo un amigo –
I go out a lot with Juan, but he's just a friend

Mi hermana esta saliendo con mi mejor amigo –
My sister is going out with my best friend

Podríamos ir todos al cine – We could all go to the cinema

Y después a pasear – And then for a walk

La primera cita – The first date

El primer beso – The first kiss

Petición de mano – Family engagement party

Nos hemos comprometido – We have got engaged

Nos casamos en julio – We're getting married in July

Son muy jóvenes – They are very young

FAMILY LIFE

Happy families

We all know how important the family is in Spain but, if you read the newspapers regularly or watch television, you could get the impression that times are changing and that the Spanish family unit might not be as strong as it used to be.

It's reported, for example, that Spain has the lowest birth rate in the world, more women are working here than in other European countries, teenagers are becoming more independent and outward-looking and more homes for the elderly are opening throughout the country.

Even so, despite these statistics, wherever you go in Spain you still see children being indulged and petted and youths walking down the street unashamedly with their arm around a younger sister or their mother or grandmother and, at weekends, restaurants are still full of whole families enjoying a meal together. *¡Viva la familia!*

Madre, padre – Mother, father

Padres – Parents

Hijo, hija – Son, daughter

Hijos – Children (sons, or sons and daughters)

Hijas – Children (daughters)

Hermana, hermano – Sister, brother

Tío, tía – Uncle, aunt

Prima – Cousin (female)

Primo – Cousin (male)

Sobrina, sobrino – Niece, nephew

Abuelo, abuela – Grandfather, grandmother

Padrino, madrina – Godfather, godmother

Compadre – Father of one's godchild or godfather of one's child

Comadre – Mother of one's godchild or godmother of one's child

Nuera, yerno – Daughter-in-law, son-in-law

Suegra, suegro – Mother-in-law, father-in-law

Consuegro, consuegra – The father, mother of one's son- or daughter-in-law

Consuegros – Plural of the above

Cuñada, cuñado – Sister-in-law, brother-in-law

Padrasto, madrastra – Stepfather, stepmother

Hermanastro – Stepbrother

Hermanastra – Stepsister

Having a baby in Spain

So you are pregnant, and when it begins to show you will probably find that the older Spanish women who used to smile at you in the street will now beam at you, shower you with congratulatory remarks, and ask such questions as *¿Quieres un niño o una niña?* – Do you want a boy or a girl?

It becomes the obvious topic of conversation and an excellent chance to practise your Spanish, particularly if you decide to prepare for the birth in Spain by attending maternity classes.

And it is perfectly acceptable for you to peer into strangers' prams and to strike up a conversation about babies – in fact, having a baby in Spain could do more for your conversational Spanish than years of classes.

Before giving birth, it might be worth your while giving the matter of location your serious consideration. The birthrate has fallen so drastically in Spain, in some rural areas they are offering cash incentives to couples willing to provide the village

(Sign on wall reads: Benomocarra pays couples 200,000 pesetas for baby number three)

"When I say no, I mean no. Not even for half a million."

with new inhabitants, not to mention the 16 weeks maternity leave for working mothers.

Estoy embarazada de tres meses – I am three months pregnant

Salgo de cuentas el veinte de febrero – The baby is due on February 20th

¿Quieres un niño o una niña? – Do you want a boy or a girl?

Un niño, para tener la parejita – A boy, then I'll have one of each (to have a pair)

¿Cómo se va a llamar? – What are you going to call it? (What will be its name?)

Ya tengo la cuna y el cochecito – I've already got the cradle and the pram

Un amigo me ha regalado una canastilla – A friend has given me a layette

El parto ha sido muy difícil, con forceps – It was a very difficult birth, with forceps

Estuve con contracciones durante varias horas – The (my) contractions went on for hours

La comadrona era más simpática que el médico – The midwife was nicer than the doctor

Mi hermana va a ser la madrina – My sister is going to be the godmother

Está de baja por maternidad – She is on maternity leave

¿La estás criando? – Are you breastfeeding her?

No tengo mucha leche, le estoy dando biberones también – I haven't got much milk, I am bottle feeding as well

¿Duerme bien? ¿Llora mucho? – Does he/she sleep well? Does he/she cry a lot?

El padre es experto en cambiar pañales - The father is an expert at changing nappies

Baby talk

It doesn't really matter of course what language you use to talk to Spanish babies. *"Coochicoochi"* probably makes as much sense to them as it does to an English baby. But talking to their parents is a different matter altogether and you will need to know some appropriate standard phrases.

If you know the family well, you will probably be encouraged to speak to the infant in English as it grows older. More and more Spanish parents are adopting the attitude that it is never too soon for their children to learn a second language.

One advantage to baby talk in Spain is you can always tell the baby's gender. The ears of baby girls are pierced and tiny gold sleepers introduced before they leave the maternity hospital, and the traditional pink for a girl and blue for a boy is still very much the custom.

¡Enhorabuena! – Congratulations!

¿Cuándo ha nacido? – When was (the baby) born?

¿Qué tiempo tiene? – How old is it (in days, weeks)

¿Cuántos años tiene? – How old is he/she? (in years)

Es una preciosidad de niña – What a lovely baby girl!

Es una preciosidad de niño – What a lovely baby boy!

Es una preciosidad – What a lovely baby!

¡Cómo se parece a la madre! – Doesn't it look like its mother!

¡Cómo se parece al padre! – Doesn't it look like its father!

¿A quién se parece el bebé? – Who does the baby look like?

Necesito pañales, biberones, chupete, un carrito – I need nappies, baby bottles, a dummy, a pushchair

Dodotis, y una cunita (Moisés) – Dodotis (trade name often used for all disposable nappies), and a cradle (Moses basket)

Su hermano tiene celos – His/her brother is jealous

¿Duerme bien? – Does (the baby) sleep well?

No, me da la noche, no duerme nunca – No, I am having bad nights, s/he never sleeps

¿Llora mucho? – Does the baby cry much?

Si, menos mal que tengo la baja por maternidad –
Yes, it's just as well that I have maternity leave

Talking to your children's friends

Unlike the old days when foreigners coming to settle in Spain were mostly retirees, the couples setting up home here these days are much younger and usually have children with them. These children have a lot of adapting to do, having to cope with new schools, new friends, a new life and a new language.

Happily, they seem to have no problem with Spanish and usually pick it up much more quickly than their parents do, especially those who go to Spanish schools. Bilingualism comes easily to the young brain – and the younger the better, it seems. I have a vivid memory of my own daughter acting as interpreter for her Spanish and English grandparents before her third birthday.

All this can leave the monolingual parents feeling a bit left out, especially if your child brings home a gang of Spanish school friends and you don't know what they are saying or might be plotting. This is a situation where it really does help to know some Spanish. If nothing else, it makes the school run more sociable and organising birthday parties a whole lot easier.

¿Cómo te va en el colegio? – How are you getting on at school?

¿Sacas buenas notas? – Do you get good marks?

¿Cúal es tu asignatura preferida? – What's your favourite subject?

¿Qué quieres ser de mayor? – What do you want to be when you grow up?

¿Tienes muchos deberes? – Have you got much homework?

¿Vives cerca de aquí? – Do you live near here?

Ahora os pongo la merienda – I'll get your tea in a minute

¿Quieres quedarte a cenar? – Would you like to stay for dinner?

¿Te gustan los huevos pasados por agua? – Do you like boiled eggs?

¿Tus padres saben que estás aqui? – Do your parents know you are here?

Nuestros hijos son compañeros de clase – Our children are class-mates

Tenemos que comprar un regalo – We have to buy a present

Me han invitado a un cumpleaños – I've been invited to a birthday party

Los otros niños de la clase se meten conmigo – The other children in the class pick on me

¿Puedo hablar con el profesor de mi hijo? – Can I speak to my son's teacher?

Soy María, la madre de Jaimito – My name is María, I am Jamie's mother

Mañana va a faltar a clase, tiene cita con el médico – He/she will miss class tomorrow, he/she has a doctor's appointment

Llegará tarde, sobre las doce – He/she will be late, around midday

"Can you spare a coin? It's my son's first communion."

IMPORTANT OCCASIONS

The first communion

When you go to your favourite restaurant or *venta* at the weekend any time during May and June you might see several long tables obviously set up for a big party. If you do, the place will be invaded at any moment by excited families and their guests, all dressed in their best and fussing over at least one little girl dressed like a miniature bride or a boy in a sailor outfit. It is First Communion time again and the majority of ten-year-olds in Spain are the centre of attention.

Every year the clergy issue pleas to families to keep the celebrations simple and meaningful, but to little effect. Most families, determined to make it a big day and to keep up with the Joneses, spend vast amounts on new outfits, gifts and banquets.

If you are invited to a First Communion in Spain, a gift will be expected. You should congratulate the communicant and, in the case of a girl, say to her *"estás guapísima."*

Voy a hacer mi primera comunión el día 10 – I am going to make my first communion on the 10th

Después vamos a celebrarlo – Afterwards we are going to celebrate

Estás invitado – You are invited

¿En qué iglesia y a qué hora? – Which church, and at what time?

A las 10, pero la misa es sólo para los familiares – At 10, but the mass is just for the relatives

Estás guapísima/o – You look lovely/very handsome

Voy de capitán – It's a captain's uniform (I am going as a captain)

Es el día más feliz de mi vida – It is the happiest day of my life

Preferimos celebrarlo en la intimidad – We prefer a (small, quiet) private celebration

No somos católicos – We are not Roman Catholics

Mi hijo no hace la comunión – My son is not going to make his first communion

¿A qué religión perteneces? – What religion are you?

Soy protestante, anglicano/a, metodista – I'm Protestant, Anglican, Methodist

Soy musulmán/a, testigo de Jehová, judía – I'm Moslem, a Jehovah's Witness, Jewish

Soy agnóstico/a, ateo/a – I´m agnostic, an atheist

"Excuse me, but haven't we got divorced
somewhere before?"

Going to a wedding

Official statistics on marriages in Spain give the impression
that few couples are bothering any more with traditional
weddings – yet the waiting list to get married in some
churches is so long you could put your name down now and
then take your time finding someone to marry. And there
are plenty of couples who take the whole thing so seriously,
especially those tying the knot in a Catholic church, they are
even willing to sign up for a pre-matrimonial training course.

If you as a foreigner are invited to a Spanish church
wedding, the first thing you notice that is different from an
English wedding is that the groom is accompanied by his
mother, *la madrina*. There is no best man. The father of the
bride hands the rings to the groom, *el novio*.

Something else that will strike you as unusual are the
flash bulbs that go off constantly throughout the ceremony.

The priest doesn't even blink when the wedding photographer and guests close in to take pictures from all angles. And nobody pays any attention to the noise made by children playing at the back of the church.

While *los novios* and witnesses are signing the register, everyone else gathers at the church entrance, waiting to throw white rice, not confetti, at the happy couple. Then it's off to the reception, which is much like a wedding anywhere except for one detail: there are no speeches.

Nos casamos el día veinte de julio – We are getting married on July 20th

Los novios van de luna de miel a Cuba – The newlyweds are going to Cuba on their honeymoon

El padre entrega a la novia – The father gives away the bride

El novio va acompañado de su madre – The bridegroom is accompanied by his mother

En mi país, el mejor amigo es quien acompaña al novio – In my country, the best friend accompanies the groom

Y organiza la despedida de solteros – And he organises the stag night (bachelors' farewell)

La despedida de solteras se hace varios días antes de la boda - The hen party (spinsters' farewell) is held several days before the wedding

El convite es en un restaurante de la costa – The reception is in a restaurant on the coast

Se casan por lo civil/por la iglesia – They are getting married in a registry office/church

Han puesto una lista de bodas en Madrid – They have a wedding list (in a shop) in Madrid

La dama de honor es una prima de la novia – The bridesmaid is the bride's cousin

¿En que iglesia se casan? – In which church are they getting married?

¡Qué guapa está la novia! – How beautiful the bride looks!

¿Habrá misa? – Will there be mass?

"Where did he work?"

Spanish funerals

If you hear a Spanish friend has died and you want to attend the funeral, you will need to be quick off the mark. You should find out immediately where the family has congregated and when the funeral is to be held, because it is likely to be in the next few hours.

Close friends and relatives usually go to the cemetery, or wherever the body is laid out, to give their condolences and spend some time with the family. It is customary for the family to stay by the body until it is time for the funeral.

The funeral service, usually with mass, is followed by interment, more often in a niche than a grave, though cremation is becoming more popular in Spain. Not everyone attends the service. It is quite acceptable to wait outside and give your condolences to the family when they emerge with the coffin. The traditional words of condolence are *te acompaño en el sentimiento*, I am with you in your sorrow.

The first funeral I went to in Spain was in a small village, where old customs still prevailed. All the men of the village attended, but very few women were there. After the service, everyone filed past the family to shake their hands and offer words of condolence. Then the family and close friends followed the coffin to the cemetery and the villagers went back to their daily routine.

Many of the men were in their working clothes but the family of course were all in black, and would probably stay in black for many years. This mourning custom is slowly dying out, though many older people still wear black for a certain period.

¿Sabes que se ha muerto tu vecino? – Have you heard that your neighbour died?

¿Cuándo es el entierro? – When is the funeral?

La misa es a las once, en la capilla del cementerio – The mass is at 11, in the cemetery chapel

El cadáver está en el tanatorio – The body is in the morgue

Te acompaño en el sentimiento – I am with you in your sorrow

Era una buena mujer/un buen hombre – She was a good woman/good man

Su marido está destrozado – Her husband is devastated

Por fin ha descansado, sufrió mucho – He/she is at rest at last, he/she suffered a lot

En paz descanse – May he/she rest in peace

Está con el Señor – He/she is with the Lord

¿Qué van a hacer con las cenizas? – What are they going to do with the ashes?

La familia tiene un columbario – The family has a niche for the urn

El duelo/el velatorio – The act of mourning, the vigil, wake

El ataúd – The coffin

Pompas fúnebres/funeraria – Funeral services

Poner una esquela en el periódico – Put a (death) notice in the newspaper

Dar el pésame – To offer condolences

Estar de luto – To be in mourning

Quiero enviar una corona – I'd like to send a wreath

SHOPPING

At the supermarket

Having set up home in Spain, one of your first trips is almost certain to be to the local supermarket and, if you want to integrate into the Spanish way of life, the items at the top of your shopping list will be olive oil, garlic, parsley and lemons – important ingredients in Spanish cooking.

You don't need to speak much Spanish in a supermarket because you can take most of what you want straight off the shelves, but when you buy meat and fish and other fresh produce you will need to explain what you want to an assistant and a phrase book or dictionary will come in handy.

If they don't have the system whereby you grab a number and wait your turn, you should ask who is the last person in the queue by saying *"¿Quién es la última?"* Somebody will say *"Yo"*, and you take your place behind that person, not forgetting to say *"Yo"* to the next customer who asks who is last in the queue. If the queue is long, it is quite acceptable to leave it for a while, but first be sure to establish your position in it.

Checkouts in small Spanish supermarkets are much more personal than those in large supermarkets. Customers often know the cashier by name and enjoy a chat while being served. Some are quite happy to extend credit to regular customers in exchange for a signature, especially in small towns and villages.

Ternera/cordero/cerdo/cabrito/despojos – Beef/ lamb/pork/kid/offal

Pavo/pollo/pato – Turkey/ chicken/duck

Carne de caza/conejo/pichón/faisán/venado – Game/rabbit/pigeon/pheasant/venison

Charcutería/jamón/embutidos – Cured meats/ ham/sausages

Jamón Serrano/jamón cocido/beicon – mountain ham/cooked ham/bacon

Pescado/mariscos – Fish/shellfish

Fresco/congelado – Fresh/frozen

Un kilo de carne picada – A kilo of minced meat

Carne para estofado – meat for stews

Filetes finos/gruesos – Fine/thick fillets

Carne troceada – meat cut into cubes

Carne deshuesada – boned meat

Pollo/pescado limpio – chicken/fish gutted

Medio kilo de manzanas – Half a kilo of apples

Un cuarto de jamón – A quarter of a kilo of ham

Cuarto y mitad de pimientos – A quarter of a kilo of peppers and half as much again

Cien gramos de pasas – 100 grams of raisins

Aceite de oliva – Olive oil

Limones/ajo/perejil – Lemons/garlic/parsley

¿Quién es la última? – Who is last in the queue?

¿Cuánto es? – How much is it?

¿Me lo apunta por favor? – Would you put it on my account please?

¿Me da más bolsas? – Would you give me some more bags?

Entrega a domicilio – Home delivery

At the ironmonger's

I'm not sure if this is a long-standing Spanish ironmongery custom or if it's just me, but *ferreterías* seem to stock a strange mix of goods. It's not the first place I would think of going to if I needed batteries or a shower curtain, but that's what I saw in the ironmonger's I went to recently – and while there I could have stocked up on light bulbs and bought a vacuum flask.

Not only is there a huge variety of goods on display, ironmongery seems to lend itself to the use of localisms – and the local word for a certain tool or appliance can be a far cry from the one found in the dictionary or learned in a Spanish class.

Matters are made worse by the fact that many of us often don't even know the name of the tool or gadget we want in any language. An ironmonger in Malaga once told me his foreign customers used mime language to get their message across and it made him feel he was involved in a game of charades.

Yes, going into a *ferretería*, especially in the old days, was quite a linguistic challenge, especially when you were looking for something out of the ordinary such as a self-tapping screw or a left-handed pipe threader.

It's much easier these days, of course. All you have to do is go to one of those huge DIY stores that are opening all over the place and take what you want off the shelf. If you have a problem, there is usually someone on hand who speaks your language.

¿Me hace una copia de esta llave? – Can you make me a copy of this key?

No sé si me va a entender – I don't know if you'll understand

Estamos haciendo trabajos de albañilería – We are doing some bricklaying work

Y me hace falta un palustre – And I need a trowel

Y lija de papel para madera y para hierro – And sandpaper for wood and metal

Y una escofina de madera – And a wood rasp

¿Cómo se venden los tornillos y los tacos? – How do you sell screws and rawlplugs?

Por unidad. ¿Cuántos quiere? – By the unit. How many do you want?

También necesito brocas, un martillo, un destornillador y un nivel – I also need drill bits, a hammer, a screwdriver, and a spirit level

Una clema de conexión y unos alicates – A strip of connectors, and pliers

Unas tenazas y una llave inglesa – Pincers and a spanner

Los extranjeros piden muchos adaptadores – Foreigners ask for a lot of adaptors

Cable paralelo, y cable manguera – Two strand electric wiring (cable), and three strand (flex)

El techo necesita una mano de pintura – The ceiling needs a coat of paint

Enchufe macho y enchufe hembra – Plug and socket

¿Tiene bombillas de bayoneta? – Have you got light bulbs with bayonet fitting?

No, aquí no hay mucha demanda – No, there's not much call for those here

Tenemos bombillas estandard o de vela, de rosca – We have standard and candle bulbs, with the screw in base

¿De cuántos watios? – How many watts?

Un taladro eléctrico (en Malaga, un guarrito) – An electric drill

Una balda de estantería (en Malaga, una batea) – A shelf

Una alcayata (en Malaga, una escarpia) – A hook

Un cáncamo (en Malaga, una brilla) – An eyebolt

Una brocha, un pincel, una llana y una espátula – A paint brush, a brush, a laying-on trowel and a scraper

Y si tiene, pilas, y disolvente – And if you have them, batteries and solvent

La cárcel - The screw clamp (*"cárcel"* is also a prison)

Un berbiquí y una garlopa - A hand drill (brace) and a trying plane

Creo que eso es todo. ¿Me presta una carretilla? – I think that's it. Can you lend me a wheelbarrow?

Buying things for the house

If you have just settled in Spain, you will most probably need to buy furniture and fittings for your new home. If you don't speak Spanish, it's advisable to go to the furniture store armed with a bilingual list carefully compiled beforehand, and a pencil and paper.

I learned the hard way the very first time I set off to buy some clothes-hangers, the one essential item missing from the apartment I had rented in Granada. I tried to explain what I wanted, with much gesticulating, to the assistant in the furniture store, but sadly my Spanish and acting techniques were not up to the task and I was offered everything from a wardrobe to a footstool.

The puzzled assistant finally offered me a pencil and paper and I managed to sketch something that was recognizably a hanger. *"¡Una percha!"* she said, with a huge smile. And then, *"No tenemos."* And sent me down the street to an ironmonger's.

Buscamos una consola para la entrada – We're looking for a hall table

Y un espejo de cuerpo entero – And a full length mirror

¿Me puede enseñar un catálogo? – Can you show me a catalogue?

¿Lo entregan en casa? ¿Cuánto puede tardar? – Do you deliver it? How long will it take?

Unos dos meses, y se lo instalamos también – About two months, and we instal it for you too

¿Vende estantes de madera? – Do you sell wooden shelves?

Sólo tenemos estanterías en forma de "kit" – We only have bookshelves in kit form

Una cabecera para una cama de ochenta centímetros – A headboard for an 80 centimetre-wide bed

¿Lo hay en otro tipo de madera? – Do you have it in any other kind of wood?

Pino, cerezo, haya, nogal, roble – Pine, cherry, beech, walnut, oak

Un mueble para el ordenador – A computer table

Una mesa auxiliar – A side table

Una lámpara de pie – A standard lamp

Un dormitorio infantil – A child's bedroom (set usually including bed, wardrobe, chest of drawers...)

¿Se vende la mesita de noche por separado? – Is the bedside table sold separately?

Una cómoda alta o antigua – A chest of drawers (tall/old fashioned, usually for a bedroom)

Una cómoda, un aparador – A chest of drawers (lower), a sideboard

Una vitrina – A display cabinet

El tocador – The dressing table

Un paragüero – An umbrella stand

Un plafón, un appliqué – A ceiling light, wall light

Ropa blanca – Household linen

Tenemos moqueta en toda la casa – We have wall to wall carpets throughout

Pero queremos también una alfombra – But we want a rug as well

Un mueble combinado, por módulos – wall units

Un carrito/un camarera – a trolley

Un perchero – a coat/hat stand

Shopping for clothes

Although you can usually pick from the clothes rail or shoe rack the things you want to try on and be fairly confident that everything in stock is also on display, there is still a lot of personal attention in the clothes shops and boutiques and you need to be able to converse with the assistant, especially when you are faced with an array of size numbers you don't understand.

The new shopping centres springing up everywhere have a lot of advantages. They make shopping for clothes much easier than traipsing all over town to find just the right boutique, they offer a wide variety of options to choose from, all under one roof and, when you're exhausted after a hard day's shopping, they provide a handy place to stop for a coffee.

¿Le puedo ayudar en algo? – Can I help you with anything?

Gracias, no, sólo estoy mirando – No thank you, I am just looking around

¿Tendría este traje en otro color? – Do you have this suit in a different colour?

¿Tiene estos zapatos en un cuarenta y tres? –
Do you have these shoes in a size 43?

Necesito una talla más grande/mas pequeño –
I need a larger/smaller size

¿Dónde puedo probarlo? – Where can I try it on?

En el probador – In the dressing room

Detrás de esta cortina – Behind this curtain

¿Me sienta bien esto? – Does this look good on me?

Le favorece mucho – It suits you very much

Le estiliza – It makes you look slim

Está de moda – It is fashionable

Me está muy justo – It is very tight

¿Se puede arreglar? – Can it be altered?

La modista lo puede hacer para el jueves –
The seamstress can do it for Thursday

Shopping for summer

Supermarket shopping is hard work at the best of times, but
in summer the idea of loading up the car and unloading it
again when you get back home is enough to make anyone
wilt. Happily, many Spanish supermarkets will now do the
main shopping for you, and deliver what you need to your
kitchen door. Just ask at your local supermarket next time
you are unloading your basket at the checkout counter.

On the other hand, shopping for sun hats, swim suits, lilo
beds, buckets and spades and other essential items for the
children, is a much more enjoyable experience – and just as
integral a part of a lazy summer day on the beach as ice
creams and sandy sandwiches

Un sombrero (de paja)/un abanico – A (straw)
hat /a fan

Un gorro/una gorra – A cap/a peaked cap

Crema bronceadora, factor diez – Suncream, factor 10

Un colchón de aire – An airbed

Un cubo y una pala – A bucket and spade

¿Qué color quieres? – What colour do you want?

Amarillo, rojo, verde, azul – Yellow, red, green, blue

Y un balón para jugar en el agua – And a ball for playing in the water

¿Quieres un helado? – Do you want an ice cream?

Prefiero un granizado de limón – I prefer an iced lemon drink

Un bikini y una toalla de playa – A bikini and a beach towel

Un traje de baño, talla cuarenta y cuatro – A bathing costume, size 44

¿Me lo puedo probar? – Can I try it on?

Si, pero con la ropa interior puesta – Yes, but with your underclothes on

¿Cuáles son los productos típicos de aquí? – What are the typical products here?

Quiero llevarme un recuerdo de Marbella – I want to get a souvenir of Marbella

¿Cuánto quiere gastar? – How much do you want to spend?

¿Quieres algo del supermercado? – Do you want anything from the supermarket?

Tomates, pepino, pimientos verdes – Tomatoes, cucumber, green peppers

Y cebollas y ajo para hacer gazpacho – And onions and garlic to make gazpacho

Lechuga y queso para una ensalada – Lettuce and cheese for a salad

Agua mineral y cerveza – Mineral water and beer

Tónica, Coca-Cola y zumos – Tonic water, Coca Cola and (fruit) juices

Vino tinto de mesa y Casera – Red table wine and Casera (lemonade-type fizz)

Para hacer tinto de verano – To make *"tinto de verano"* (refreshing red wine drink)

No tengo ganas de comer en verano – I don't feel like eating in summer

¿Tiene servicio a domicilio? – Do you do home deliveries?

Si, por un gasto mínimo de cuarenta euros – Yes, if you spend a minimum of 40 euros

The January sales

January in Spain is likely to bring moans and mention of the *cuesta de enero* – a cuesta being a slope and, implicitly in this expression, an uphill one. Everyone spent too much during the Christmas season and now it is a huge struggle to get to the end of January.

Help in climbing the January slope comes with the January sales, which in Spain start on the seventh, the day after the Three Wise Men have delivered the goods. Taking back unwanted gifts and exchanging them for articles on sale at a discount can really lighten the load...

The problem with the sales though is the same as anywhere – jostling crowds, packed changing rooms and surly overworked shop assistants. And when you finally find what you want, they haven't got it in your size.

"Stand aside - it's a stampede."

La cuesta de enero – The January slope (struggle to get through January financially)

Las rebajas de enero – The January sales

La mejor oferta, la mejor ganga – The best offer, the best bargain

Rebajas – Sales

Rebajado – Reduced

Liquidación – Everything must go, clearance

Existencias limitadas – Limited stock

Tres por dos – Three for the price of two

Oferta – On offer

A mitad de precio – Half price

Descuento – Discount

Ganga – Bargain

¿Cuánto es? ¿Cuánto cuesta? – How much is it? How much does it cost?

No hay de mi talla – They haven't got my size.

¿Tiene esto en una cuarenta y seis? – Have you got this in a 46?

Si no hay expuesto, es que no lo hay – If it's not displayed, we haven't got it

¿Dónde están los probadores? – Where are the changing rooms?

¿Esto es la cola para los probadores? – Is this the queue for the changing rooms?

¿Quién es el última? – Who is last? (in the queue)

Señora, lo máximo son cinco prendas – Madam, you can only take five articles in

¡Vaya chollo de camisa! – This shirt was a real find

Pague aquí – Pay here

¿Tiene otra talla? – Do you have another size?

Centro Comercial – Shopping centre

Hay una cola larguísima – There's a very long queue

Me está pisando – You're treading on my foot

¿No tiene cambio? – Haven't you got any change?

¿Le importa sellar la garantía? – Could you stamp the guarantee?

¿Hay donde sentarse? – Is there anywhere I can sit down?

Estoy agotado/a – I am exhausted

"And detoxify what we are about to receive... amen."

F O O D

Mediterranean diet

For many years – decades, in fact - Spaniards were told that their regular diet, with all its bean stews, bread and lashings of oil, was making them fat. They might like what they were eating, but it was held to be about as good for them as the English diet was considered to be tasty.

Then along came the nutritionists and chefs telling us that olive oil is healthier than butter, that sardines are good for reducing cholesterol levels, and pulses are not only cheap but nutritious too. As for fresh fish, fruit and vegetables, basic ingredients of the Mediterranean diet, you can't eat too much of them.

Now, just when we all agree that the Mediterranean diet is the best for us, we hear that Spain's lifestyle has changed so much that housewives have less time to prepare meals and more and more of them are buying processed foods from the supermarket instead of fresh produce at their local market.

The weekly shopping trip to the supermarket is taking hold, and the freezer and fast food are coming into their own. Big family meals at midday are being relegated to the weekend only, and those who go out to work are eating in restaurants. Fortunately, there are still plenty of restaurants serving bean stews and salads with lashings of olive oil.

La dieta mediterránea es muy sana – The Mediterranean diet is very healthy

Se usa mucho aceite de oliva – It uses a lot of olive oil

Fruta fresca, verduras, comida casera – Fresh fruit, vegetables, home-made food

Antes, el congelador era para hacer hielo – The freezer used to be for making ice

Las amas de casa ya no van todos los días al mercado – Housewives no longer go to the market every day

La venta de productos frescos ha caído – The sale of fresh produce has dropped

Los jóvenes prefieren *"el fast food"* o sea, la comida rápida – Young people prefer fast food (and sometimes call it *"el fast food"*)

Hay menos tiempo para cocinar – There is less time to cook

El puchero necesita varias horas – Making stock takes several hours

Muchas parejas comen fuera de casa – Many couples eat out

Los guisos son para el fin de semana – Cooked meals are for the weekend

Por la noche como un yogur, una manzana – In the evening I eat a yoghourt, an apple

Queso, fiambres, ensalada, un bocadillo – Cheese, cold meats, salad, a sandwich

Una hamburguesa, una pizza, un huevo frito – A hamburger, a pizza, a fried egg

Comida por encargo, a domicilio – Food (ordered) to take away, home delivery

Meals and meal times

Eating habits, like everything else, are changing in Spain, but generally speaking at least one meal a day is still a family affair – and Spaniards still eat later than most other Europeans.

Few Spaniards eat breakfast at home. They will either grab a coffee and toast on the way to work or, if they can take a break, have a more leisurely breakfast in a bar around ten or eleven. It's likely they will be back in the bar for a beer or glass of wine and a *tapa* on their way home for lunch. Children might go to school on a glass of milk but in the school bag there will be a snack to eat during the morning break.

Lunch, between two and three, is usually the big meal of the day and runs to at least three courses, starting in summer with a salad or egg dish and in winter with a hearty soup and stew. An afternoon snack called the *merienda*, usually consisting of a sizeable sandwich, keeps Spaniards going until dinner time, which appears on the table around nine or ten or even later in the summer. Though less substantial than lunch, *la cena* is still a meal to be reckoned with.

Desayuno/almuerzo/merienda/cena – Breakfast/lunch/tea/dinner

Tapa – Small snack served with a glass of beer or wine

Bocadillo (bocata) – Sandwich

Sandwich - Toasted sandwich

Café - Coffee

Café con leche – White coffee

Café cortado – Coffee with only a little milk

Café sombra – Coffee with a lot of milk

Bollos – Buns in general

Galletas – Biscuits

Refresco – Soft drink

¿Qué quieres desayunar/comer/merendar/ cenar? – What would you like for breakfast/ lunch/tea/dinner?

Not by bread alone

When time is dragging, a Spaniard might use the expression *más largo que un día sin pan* (longer than a day without bread), which implies how painful it is to go without bread in this country. The Spanish of course are a nation of bread lovers. You can't have a meal or a snack here without bread.

For breakfast, it's toasted and slathered with pork dripping, with or without paprika, or doused in olive oil and possibly scraped with a clove of garlic for good measure. For snacks between meals, all kinds of cheeses, hams and sausages are stuffed into giant bread rolls, and a basketful of bread is an essential accompaniment to any meal.

Being such an important part of daily life, it's not surprising that the word bread pops up so often in Spanish conversation.

Pan de molde – Sliced sandwich bread

Pan integral – Brown (wholemeal) bread

Pan cateto – Rough textured country bread

Una barra de Viena – A long French-like loaf

Una rebanada de pan – A slice of bread

Un bollo/bollito – A bread roll/little roll

Pan de los Angeles – Communion wafer

Pásate por la panadería – Pop by the bakery

Lo que más me gusta es la corteza – The crust is the bit I like

Media docena de bollitos y un pan de molde – Half a dozen rolls and a sliced loaf (usually wrapped)

Pan rallado para freír unos filetes – Breadcrumbs for frying with slices of meat

¿Me lo puede cortar? – Can you slice it for me?

¿Vende levadura? – Do you sell yeast?

Contigo pan y cebolla – You're all I need

Se vende como pan caliente – It sells like hot cakes

No sólo de pan vive el hombre – Man cannot live by bread alone

Al pan, pan, y al vino, vino – To call a spade a spade

El pan nuestro de cada día – Our daily bread

Los errores son el pan nuestro de cada día – Mistakes are an everyday occurrence

Mi niña es más buena que el pan - My little girl is as good as gold

Ganarse el pan – To earn a living

"And I'll have prawns without boric acid, *chanquetes* without urine, and then you can bring me the bill without inflation."

EATING OUT

At the restaurant

One of the delights of living on the *Costas* is eating out, almost as often as you feel like it, at restaurants and bars catering for every taste and pocket. You can take your choice, from well-appointed gourmet restaurants to the popular *ventas* packed, particularly at weekends, with large and boisterous Spanish families tucking into country fare and having a great time.

Favourite places to eat, especially in summer of course, are the *chiringuitos*, the cheap and cheerful beach restaurants serving *pescaíto frito* or delicious fried fish, usually fresh. You can walk into one of these straight from the beach. I know one where the waiters don't bother taking orders but rush around with dishes of squid or sardines or whatever, shouting "Who wants this?" When it's time to pay, they count the plates piled up on your table.

At the end of the meal, in an informal atmosphere, you might hear a Spaniard ask the waiter for *la dolorosa*. This is not an exotic liqueur but literally means "the painful one" and refers to the bill.

Venta – Inn, usually in the country providing cheap and hearty cooking

Una mesa para dos por favor – A table for two, please

¿Qué es lo que hay? – What's on the menu today?

¿Me trae la carta? – Would you bring the menu?

¿Qué prefieres comer, carne o pescado? – What do you want to eat, meat or fish?

¿Qué me recomienda? – What do you recommend?

Puede tomar nota – We're ready to order

De primero, una ensalada – I'll have a salad first

De segundo, estofado – Then a stew

Y de postre tomaré fruta – And for dessert I'll have fruit

¿Y para beber? – What will you have to drink?

Vino tinto/vino blanco/una cerveza – Red wine/white wine/beer

Tinto de verano – Red wine mixed with lemonade, in summer

¿Nos trae una jarra de agua? – Could you bring us a jug of water?

57

¿Cómo le gusta la carne? – How do you like your meat done?

Poco hecha – Rare

En su punto – Medium

Muy hecha – Well done

¿Qué tiene de postre? – What is there for dessert?

¿Tenéis postres caseros? – Do you have homemade desserts?

La sopa está fría – The soup is cold

¿Me trae la cuenta, por favor? – Would you bring the bill, please?

¿Está incluído el servicio? – Is service included?

Something fishy

When I eat out with Spanish friends, we often end up eating fish at a beach restaurant, which is not really surprising when you consider that Spaniards are the biggest fish-eaters in Europe. Unless of course it happens to be Monday, which is considered to be a bad day to eat fish in a restaurant because it is unlikely the fishermen have been out fishing the day before.

A problem with beach restaurants for non-Spanish speakers is that the menu, if it exists, doesn't really mean much. As soon as the paper tablecloth, basket of bread and cutlery rolled up in paper serviettes have been put in place, the waiter will reel off a list of what's available. He will highlight the fish dishes and probably omit to mention any side dishes such as salads, but these will almost certainly be available.

Vamos a un chiringuito – Let's go to a beach bar

Pescado y mariscos – Fish and seafood, shellfish

¿Qué pescado tenéis hoy fresco? – What fresh fish do you have today?

Tenemos gambas, cocidas y a la plancha – We've got prawns, boiled or grilled

Y langostinos y gambas de Malaga – and giant prawns and Malaga prawns (paler and more expensive),

Hay rosada, frito o a la plancha, con alioli – Wolf fish, for frying or grilled, with garlic mayonnaise

Pez espada - Swordfish

Pulpo (a la gallega) – Octopus (*"a la gallega"* is with boiled potatoes and paprika)

Lenguado, mero, salmonete – Sole, grouper, red mullet

Calamares, calamaritos, chopitos – Squid, baby squid, whole baby squid

Espetos (de sardinas) – Fish grilled on a stick (usually sardines)

Mejillones, almejas, coquinas – Mussels, clams, cockles

Una jarra de cerveza y seis vasos – A jug of beer and six glasses

Una botella de tinto y otra de Casera - A bottle of red wine and one of *Casera* (sweetened fizz to add to the wine)

Boquerones en vinagre o frito – Anchovies in vinegar or fried

Chanquetes – Baby fish (banned by law so don't accept them if offered)

Arroz – Rice (usally means *"paella"*)

Ensalada mixta – Mixed salad

Ensaladilla de pimientos asados – Roasted red pepper salad

Going out for breakfast

Spaniards like to have breakfast in a bar. It's not unusual to phone your bank manager or lawyer some time between ten and eleven and be told he is out having breakfast. In a breakfast bar you can always be sure of a good strong coffee. But you will need to know what to ask for. The usual *café solo*, black coffee, and *café con leche*, coffee with milk, are not your only choices. You can also ask for *a sombra*, more milk than coffee, or *a cortado*, more coffee than milk. I once saw a poster on the wall of a Malaga breakfast bar showing at least a dozen variations.

More and more Spanish bars are serving up eggs and bacon to please foreigners these days but the usual breakfast fare is *tostada*, toast, with just about anything you could wish for on it, including oil, garlic, mashed tomato, bacon, ham, a Spanish version of dripping and, yes, even butter and marmalade.

Café solo/con leche – Black coffee/with milk

Café mitad/cortado/sombra – half coffee, half milk/ more coffee/more milk

Café doble – Large coffee

Un café descafeinado de máquina – Decaffeinated coffee made in the machine

En vaso/taza – In a glass/cup

¿Podría echar un poco de leche fría? – Could you add a little cold milk?

Con leche desnatada – With skimmed milk

Un zumo de naranja – Orange juice

Tostada con mantequilla y mermelada – Toast with butter and jam

¿De pan de molde, o pan de viena? – Sliced bread, or Spanish baguette?

Un bocadillo de jamón serrano – Serrano ham sandwich

Un mollete (tostado) con aceite – A soft bread bun with olive oil

Un pitufo con jamón cocido – A small roll with ham

Un bollito con tomate restregado y ajo – A roll with scraped tomato and garlic

Un mollete con atún y pimientos morrones – A soft roll with tuna fish and red peppers

Beicon con huevo frito y salchichas – Bacon with fried egg and sausages

Una torta de aceite – A local oily flat cake

Un donut y una magdalena – A doughnut and a sponge cake (individual)

Un xuxo y una palmera – A cream-filled sugary long doughnut and a heart-shaped pastry

Chocolate con churros – Hot chocolate with a Spanish version of donuts

Churros para cuatro – *"Churros"* for four

Un croissant y un suizo – A croissant and a sugar bun

Una loca and una caracola – A round pastry with icing (typical of Malaga) and a Danish pastry (swirly)

Un colacao y galletas para los niños – Chocolate milk and biscuits for the children

Tapas

I ate my first ever *tapa* in Granada, on my first full day in Spain. I was in a bar with a fellow student celebrating our arrival in the city. Our drinks were served with a small dish of croquettes. We told the waiter we hadn't ordered any food. He explained that *a tapa* was served free with a drink whether it was ordered or not.

When we confessed we didn't know what a *tapa* was, he very kindly took it upon himself to educate us. He served us a plateful of peanuts, followed by a small dish of mushrooms in tomato sauce with bread to dip in the sauce, two slices of *salchichón* with more bread, anchovies in vinegar, potato salad and some olives. And all this without us having to order more drinks.

It was our first and most invaluable lesson as students in Spain, and the second lesson we learned soon after was that students in Granada seldom went to restaurants. If they drank enough, they could eat free. I'm happy to say there are still many bars in that wonderful city that serve free *tapas*.

¿Qué vas a tomar? – What are you going to have?

Una caña/un vino tinto/un tinto de verano – A glass of beer/red wine/red wine with lemonade

¿Qué tiene de tapa? – What *tapas* have you got?

Tenemos huevos rellenos, magro con tomate – We've got stuffed eggs, pork in tomato sauce...

Morcilla, tortilla española, albóndigas – black pudding, Spanish omelette, meat balls...

Aceitunas, patatas fritas, cacahuetes, almendras – Olives, crisps, peanuts, almonds

Ensaladilla rusa, boquerones en vinagre – Potato salad, anchovies in vinegar (and garlic)

O le puedo poner media ración de queso – Or I can give you a half portion of cheese

Una ración de ibéricos, para compartir – A portion of cured ham and sausages, to share

De cocina, tenemos fabada – The cook has made bean stew...

Y albóndigas caseras – and home-made meatballs

Una tabla de ahumados – A wooden platter of smoked fish

¿Me puede poner más pan para mojar en la salsa? – Could I have some more bread, to dip in the sauce?

AT YOUR SERVICE

At the bank

Banking is not something I feel especially well equipped to talk about. I am very good at getting money from cash machines and have embraced internet banking facilities with great relief, but I have never quite got the hang of dealing with banks or got used to their opening hours and long queues.

I do know that banks are open in the mornings and are closed at weekends and holidays. What I don't understand is where those long queues come from if they are only open when the vast majority of people are at work. And why are only one or two employees dealing with the queues while several others are sitting at their desks seemingly doing nothing?

There are other things that mystify me about banks, especially one. Why do money transfers from one country to another take so long, even when I bypass the queues and do it myself electronically? I asked my bank this when ten days had gone by and my daughter in Manchester was on the verge of starvation.

The answer, despite my long experience with the way things work here, was unexpected. I was told my instructions had gone straight from my computer to the bank's central system in Madrid, where they were printed out and then faxed to my branch in Malaga, where the person who deals with transfers was off work for a day or two, and when he got back the fax was nowhere to be found.

¿A cuánto está el cambio de libras a euros? – What is the exchange rate for pounds to euros?

Quisiera cambiar mil dólares – I'd like to change a thousand dollars

Sigo calculando en pesetas – I still calculate in pesetas

¿Me presta la calculadora? – Would you lend me the calculator?

¿Está en esta cola? – Are you in this queue?

Si, pero es la cola para cobrar la pensión – Yes, but it is the queue for getting your pension

Quiero que me cuente todo este cambio – I'd like you to count up all this small change

Póngame la cartilla al día – Update my savings book

Ingréseme este dinero en cuenta – Put this money in my account

¿Puedo contratar una caja de seguridad? – Can I rent a safe deposit box?

¿Me da un extracto de la cuenta? – Can you give me a statement?

Me han descontado algo que no corresponde – I've been charged for something that's not mine

Me hace falta un talonario/un préstamo – I need a cheque book/a loan

Quiero domiciliar el recibo del agua/electricidad/ teléfono – I want to make a standing order to pay the water bill/electricity/telephone

Quiero sacar dinero – I'd like to take some money out

La tarjeta no funciona – My card doesn't work

Quiero invertir en un fondo – I'd like to invest in a fund

Necesito una hipoteca – I need a mortgage

¿Dónde está el departamento de extranjeros? – Where is the foreigners' department?

Han devuelto este talón – This cheque has bounced

No hay fondos en su cuenta – There are no funds in your account

Estoy en números rojos – I am in the red

Quiero hablar con el director – I want to speak to the director

"Put your tongues out and march quickly past to the exit."

A visit to the doctor

This is probably one of the most alarming scenarios you can imagine as a non-Spanish speaker. You are in pain and feel sure you have some life-threatening condition and, after spending two hours in the waiting room breathing in other people's germs, you are face to face with a doctor who doesn't speak a word of English and you just know he is going to give you a flat two minutes to explain to him why you are there.

Fortunately these days this scenario doesn't happen too often, especially in places where foreigners tend to settle in Spain. Either you would go to one of the many English-speaking doctors available or take advantage of the interpreter service

65

that seems to be a fixed feature now in most Spanish hospitals and health clinics.

Of course you might decide to take the matter in your own hands and go to bed with a hot whisky – or whatever your favourite home remedy might be – and stay there until you feel better. Whatever you do, learning a few key medical phrases in Spanish could be useful, especially in an emergency.

It's best to be prepared. Don't go to the clinic armed only with those key medical phrases, but also take along all your health-related documents and insurance policies (you might not need them but it's better to err on the side of caution). And *"que te mejores"* – get better soon.

Bueno, cuénteme – Well now, tell me all about it

Dígame, ¿qué le pasa? – Tell me what's wrong with you

¿Está tomando algún medicamento? – Are you taking any medicines?

¿Está embarazada? – Are you pregnant?

¿Tiene alguna alergia? – Do you have any allergies?

¿Tiene seguro médico? – Do you have any medical insurance?

Me duele (mucho) la pierna/el hombro/el oído – My leg/shoulder/ear hurts (a lot)

Tengo fiebre – I've got a high temperature

No puedo dormir – I can't sleep

No puedo respirar – I can't breathe

Mi hijo se cayó por la escalera – My son fell down the stairs

Se ha lastimado (mucho) – He has hurt himself (a lot)

Se ha cortado – He has cut himself

Tendremos que hacer una radiografía – We´ll have to take an X-ray

Le vamos a poner unos puntos – We'll give him a few stitches

No es nada grave – It's nothing serious

Le voy a recetar unos antibióticos – I'll give you a prescription for some antibiotics

Tome un comprimido tres veces al día – Take one tablet three times a day

Estoy mareado/a – I feel dizzy

Habrá que intervenir – You'll have to have an operation

Tengo náusea - I feel sick

At the pharmacy

Years ago I knew a Spanish pharmacy where your purchases were placed in a small carrier bag emblazoned with the words, in Spanish: "Your pharmacist is a professional. Don't bother your doctor, ask your pharmacist."

The times when you could buy a wide range of medicines without a prescription are long gone, though many Spaniards still see the pharmacy as a quick alternative to a visit to the doctor – and you can still find yourself in a queue behind people discussing their ailments and symptoms with the chemist.

There is always at least one pharmacy on duty for emergencies outside normal business hours in most towns nowadays. If you should need one in the middle of the night or on a Sunday or holiday, consult the duty chemist *(farmacia de guardia)* list displayed in the window of your nearest chemist.

Farmacia – Dispensing chemist

Parafarmacia – Shop selling pharmaceutical supplies

Farmacia de guardia – Duty chemist

No se lo puedo dar sin receta – I can't give you it without a prescription

"My round today"... "No no, my income is higher than yours"... "Lets go halves then... A packet of aspirin for me and a suppository for my friend."

Necesito aspirina infantil – I need children's aspirin

¿Cómo me lo tomo? – How do I take it?

¿Prefiere cápsulas o supositorios? – Do you prefer capsules or suppositories?

Comprimidos – Tablets

¿Cual es el peso ideal para un bebé de siete meses? – What should a seven month old baby weigh?

¿Está comiendo bien? – Is she eating well?

No tengo ese jarabe para la tos ahora mismo – I haven't got that cough syrup at the moment

Tendré que pedirlo – I'll have to order it

Para esta tarde – It'll be here this afternoon

Un botiquín de primeros auxilios – A first aid kit

Una caja de condones – A packet of condoms

¿De tres o de doce? – Three or twelve?

Un test de embarazo – A pregnancy test

¿Me toma la tensión? – Would you take my blood pressure?

Algún producto para adelgazar – Something to help me slim

Health care

Until quite recently, everybody covered by the Social Security system was attached to the *ambulatorio*, a kind of out-patients centre, nearest to their home. Unlike hospital treatment under the Social Security, these had a poor reputation and were often likened to conveyor belts. Many Spaniards took their minor ailments to the casualty departments at the big hospitals, rather than wait hours for a two-minute consultation at the *ambulatorio*.

Times have changed and most *ambulatorios* have now been replaced by *centros de salud*, neighbourhood health centres, which appear to work better and focus more on preventative medicine. They offer general surgeries, antenatal and family planning clinics, and the doctors make home visits. Here all the doctors are General Practitioners or *Médicos de Familia*, and each has a quota of patients and deals with entire families, so that there is an element of continuity.

Foreigners who pay for private medical care or have medical insurance can, of course, choose a doctor who speaks English – but the good news for the many expatriates who rely on the Social Security system is the growing number of volunteer interpreters you find nowadays in hospitals and health clinics.

As we mentioned in A Visit to the Doctor, it's still a good idea to know a few medical phrases, especially in an emergency.

Seguridad social – Social Security

Centro de Salud – Health centre

Receta – Prescription

Consulta – Surgery

Urgencias – Casualty

Cartilla – Social Security card

Médico de Familia (de cabecera) – Family practitioner

Enfermera – Nurse

ATS (Asistente Técnico Sanitario) – Similar to nurse

Celador – Attendant manning the reception and enquiries desk

"I want to take someone off the waiting list."

Cita previa – Appointment

Aviso domiciliario – Request for a home visit

At the hairdresser

Going to the *peluquería* or hairdresser is a very popular pastime in Spain – and all you have to do to prove it is count the number of salons in your part of town. This plethora of *peluquerías* means you can often get your hair done without making an appointment. You can do what Spanish women often do; pop in and ask how long you have to wait and, if it's too long to hang around, you can fill in the time by doing a bit of shopping.

Unlike most women, I used to hate going to the hairdresser's, but since finding a *peluquería* that not only sends me home better coiffed but also much better informed, I rather enjoy having my hair done. My hairdresser makes it unnecessary for me to pick up one of the gossip magazines lying around. She likes to talk and gives me all the latest gossip – on her family, the neighbours, the titled, rich and famous – and keeps me right up-to-date with what's hot on the telly.

Fascinating stuff, but I must admit I still have quite a way to go before I become what one of my colleagues calls a *señora de peluquería* – a lady who is always perfectly permed and coiffed and looking as if she has just stepped out of a magazine herself.

¿Hay mucha gente esperando? – Are there many people waiting?

Voy a hacer unos recados y ahora vengo, ¿vale? – I'll go and do some errands and be right back, OK?

Lavar y peinar – A wash and blow dry

Iluminaciones, mechas – Highlights, streaks

¿Se va a cortar también? – Are you going to have it cut as well?

Sólo las puntitas – Just the ends (a trim)

Con capas – Layered

Pase aquí que le vamos a lavar la cabeza – Come over here, we'll wash your hair

¿Quiere una revista? – Would you like a magazine?

¿Cómo quiere que la peine? – How would you like me to style it?

Informal, con las puntas hacia adentro – A casual style, with the ends turned under

Y la raya a la izquierda – And the parting on the left

El flequillo más pegado a la cara – The fringe closer to my face

Defilar para suavizar las puntas – To feather the ends

Ahora mismo vienen a secarle – Someone will be along now to dry your hair

Quiero un color/tinte más rubio – I want a fairer colour/dye

Le doy el champú de color – I'll use the shampoo for coloured hair

¿Le pongo crema? – Would you like some conditioner on it?

¿Qué le parece cómo ha quedado? – What do you think? Are you happy with it?

Está guapísima – You look wonderful

Gracias. Esto es para la chica que me lavó – Thank you. This is for the girl who washed my hair.

Help in the home

"Un trabajo poco deseado" – a job that's little wanted – was the headline of an article in a Spanish newspaper recently and referred to the position of home helps or cleaning women – or

"Don't tell me your wife is out getting fulfilled,too!"

maids, as some people still call them.

Home help in Spain is called *servicio doméstico* and a woman who does this kind of work is known as *la asistenta, la mujer de limpieza* or even *la chacha*, a diminutive of the word *muchacha* meaning girl, which sounds derogatory and is the reason why some of the women interviewed in the article felt their work was degrading.

Spanish women now prefer to do other work and more and more home help jobs are being filled by immigrant workers. The first influx of Philippine women a few years back was following by a wave of Moroccan women and now it seems a lot of households are employing East Europeans.

Gone are the days when most expatriates could afford a fulltime maid, but many still hire a woman to clean the house once or twice a week. If you live in a village or small town, you can find a house cleaner by talking to your neighbours or local shopkeepers. In bigger towns, you would most likely advertise for help or go to an agency and end up with an immigrant worker rather than a Spaniard. Cleaners should be properly contracted, insured and covered by social security payments, but this is not as onerous as it sounds. Special conditions apply to domestic help and if the cleaner is part-time and works for several families, she is responsible for her own social security payments.

Se necesita mujer para limpiar – Cleaning woman wanted

Imprescindible informes – Must have references

¿Conoces a alguien que quiera trabajar? – Do you know anybody who wants a job?

¿Por horas, o día completo? – By the hour, or full time?

¿Interna o externa? – Living in, or out?

¿Tiene que saber cocinar? – Does she have to know how to cook?

¿Tiene que cuidar niños? – Does she have to look after children?

¿Paga el desplazamiento? – Do you pay transport costs?

Cobran entre tres y seis euros a la hora – They earn between three and six euros per hour

¿En qué consiste el trabajo? – What does the job entail?

Necesito alguien para hacer los trabajos más pesados – I need somebody to do the heavy work

Y para la plancha – And to iron

Hacer la compra por la mañana – To do the shopping in the morning

Hacer la comida, y dejar la cena preparada – Make lunch, and leave dinner ready

Tiene que recoger los niños del colegio – You have to collect the children from school

Y darles la merienda – And give them their tea

Vigilar que hagan los deberes – Make sure they do their homework

Limpiar toda la casa – Clean all the house

Y limpiar a fondo una vez por semana – And clean thoroughly once a week

Retirando los muebles – Pulling out all the furniture

Quedarse por las noches cuando queremos salir – Stay overnight when we want to go out

¿Cuándo puede empezar? – When can you start?

¿Le importa que le conteste mañana? – Can I give you an answer tomorrow?

Tengo más entrevistas – I have some more interviews

Le llamaré – I'll ring you.

Getting a gardener

If you must have a garden, by far the best thing is to get a gardener to go with it – one who won't waste time and money planting a delicate lawn where the full blast of salt-laden gales will destroy it. You do, however, need to check the gardener's credentials or you may end up with one who dumps cartloads of beans on your doorstep but is averse to growing anything that can't be eaten.

Gardeners tend to advertise their services on shop notice boards and on flimsy bits of paper thrust into letterboxes. Probably a more reliable way to find one is by word of mouth. Ask your friends or neighbours to recommend one.

If you should want the pleasures of a garden without all the bother you can always buy into one of those home complexes with a communal garden and pool.

¿Conoces algún jardinero que trabaje por aquí? – Do you know of a gardener who works round here?

¿Por horas, o tiempo completo? – By the hour, or full time?

Quiero que plante buganvilla – I'd like you to plant bougainvillea

Y jazmín, cerca de la casa – And jasmine, near the house

Quisiera tener frutales en el jardín – I'd like to have fruit trees in the garden

Pero también flores para cortar – But also flowers for cutting

No hace falta invernadero aquí en la costa – There is no need for a greenhouse, here on the coast

En el interior el clima es muy distinto – Inland the climate is very different

Un jardín de fácil mantenimiento – An easily maintained garden

Quitar las malas hierbas del jardín – To weed the garden

El terreno es muy malo, necesita fertilizante – The ground is very poor, it needs fertilizer

La tierra está muy seca – The soil is very dry

El cortacésped está en el cuarto de herramientas – The lawn-mover is in the tool shed

Necesito una pala y un rastrillo – I need a spade and a rake

¿Puede instalar un regador? – Can you install a sprinkler?

Regar con la manguera tarda mucho – Watering with the hosepipe takes a long time

Tendrá que mantener la piscina también – You will have to maintain the pool too

Home repairs

A major grouse among expats is you can hardly ever get a plumber or electrician when you need one. You have a leak in the house and you're desperate. You plead with the plumber to come straight away. He can't. You make an appointment for the following day. You wait at home all day and he doesn't show up. What's really galling is when he finally shows up some days later and you are not at home.

I'm told the reason for this sorry state of affairs is that all the electricians, plumbers, painters, carpenters and other handymen are far too busy. They can't cope with the population explosion along the Mediterranean coast.

Perhaps for this reason some companies are beginning to offer emergency services. I called one three days ago when my oven broke down. I'm still waiting.

Una avería – A breakdown.

El microondas está averiado – The microwave doesn't work.

Necesito un electricista/un fontanero/un pintor – I need an electrician/plumber/painter

¿Cuál es el problema? – What is the problem?

Tiene un escape – It is leaking

¿Qué le pasa? – What is the matter with it?

No se enciende, no se calienta – It won't turn on, it doesn't heat up

El tambor de la lavadora no da vueltas – The drum in the washing machine doesn't go round

Es una lavadora/un lavavajillas/un horno – It is a washing machine/dishwasher/oven

Un calentador/una placa solar/la calefacción central – A heater/solar panel/central heating

¿Qué modelo es el aparato? – What model is it (the apparatus)?

Tiene que pagar el desplazamiento – You will have to pay a call-out charge

La mano de obra, a tanto por hora – Labour charges, by the hour

Y las piezas necesarias para la reparación – And any spares needed to repair it

Tienen garantía de seis meses – They are guaranteed for six months

¿Está bajo garantía? – Is it under guarantee?

¿El mando/interruptor funciona? ¿Está enchufado? – Does the control/switch work? Is it plugged in?

La casa esta inundada – The house is flooded

Le llamarán dentro de cuarenta y ocho horas – Someone will call you (back) within 48 hours

Pasarán por su casa el mes que viene. Por la mañana – They will be there next month. In the morning

COMMUNICATING

On the phone

The first time you use the phone to speak to somebody in Spanish can be an alarming experience. There is no way you can revert to sign language if you suddenly become speechless, and the person at the other end can hang up before you finally manage to string a sentence together.

I've never forgotten the first phone call I made in Spain. It got very complicated. It was from a public phone box in Granada where I was looking for somewhere to live. I was holding the phone, a newspaper open at the "apartments for rent" page, some coins, a pen and a scrap of paper, when a voice barked *"Diga"* down the line and totally unnerved me.

I managed to convey to her what I wanted and she agreed I could look at her apartment. I asked for directions and naturally she asked me where I was. I hadn't the faintest idea. I had to open the door of the phone box and ask the queue of people waiting patiently outside, *"¿Dónde estoy?"* – "Where am I?"

¿Puedo usar el teléfono? – May I use the phone?

Es una llamada local – It's a local call

Le atiende el servicio de información de Telefónica – This is directory enquiries

¿Me puede facilitar el número de un restaurante en Perth, Australia? – Can you give me the number of a restaurant in Perth, Australia?

Para información internacional tiene que marcar el diez veinticinco – For international directory enquiries you have to dial 11825

Diga – Hello? Yes?

Le atiende el contestador automático – This is an answer phone

Deje su mensaje después de oir la señal – Leave your message after the beep

Si quiere información, pulse el uno – If you want information, press 1

Si desea dejar un mensaje o enviar un fax, pulse dos – If you would like to leave a message or send a fax, press 2

Le atiende Juan José. ¿En qué puedo ayudarle? – This is Juan José speaking, how can I help you?

¿De dónde me llama? – Where are you calling from?

¿Le importaría hablar más despacio? – Would you mind speaking more slowly?

¿Me pone con la extensión treinticinco? – Would you put me through to extension 35?

¿Me pone con la persona encargada? – Would you put me through to the person in charge?

Letter-writing

Years ago in England, students struggling with the Spanish language were taught a list of expressions to use in letter writing that struck them as being down right antiquated, to put it mildly. They found it quite amazing that someone should end a letter with such flowery phrases as *"Sin otra particular, reciba, junto al testimonio de mi consideración personal más distinguida, un saludo muy cordial".*

These days you can sign off a Spanish business letter with nothing more than *"Un saludo muy cordial"* – though some of the old formality still remains. Whereas in an English letter we address all and sundry as "Dear" so-and-so, a Spaniard would only use the word *"Querido"* when writing to a close friend. In a formal letter you would open with, *"Muy señor mio"* or *"Estimada señora"* and when writing to an acquaintance rather than a friend you would probably say *"Apreciado amigo"*

In signing off a letter, the Spanish and English terms used

"The post looks to be getting better darling - here's cousin Amparo's Christmas card from 2000."

are similar – from the formal *"saluda atentamente"* through the friendly *"un saludo"* to the more intimate *"Un abrazo"* and *"Besos"*.

Querido Jorge – Dear George

Queridos padres – Dear mum and dad

¿Cómo estáis? – How are you all?

Por aquí todo va bien – All's well here

Recuerdos a ... – Remember me to...

Espero verte pronto – Hoping to see you soon

Un abrazo/besos – A hug/kisses (to end a letter)

Afectuosamente – Affectionately yours

Estimada Señora – Dear Madam

Muy señor mío – Dear Sir

Adjunto le remito – I enclose herewith

Adjunto – I enclose

Un saludo – Yours,

Esperando tener noticias suyas – Hoping to hear from you

Acusamos recibo de su carta – We acknowledge receipt of your letter

Le saluda atentamente – Yours sincerely or yours faithfully

En espera de haberles correspondido – Hoping this meets with your approval

On-line

The language of computers and the internet is fairly easy to get to grips with in Spanish. If the English word is not adopted in its entirety, the translation into Spanish is likely to be so similar as to make little difference.

Net-savvy young Spaniards talk quite happily about banners, bits and backups (pronounced *"bakoop"*) and many of them prefer to say emails rather than *"emilios"* and *"spam"* instead of *"correo basura."*

"La red" is the Spanish word for the web, but you're more likely to hear your Spanish friends use the word *"el web"*. The English word "chat" has been turned into a new verb– *"chatear"* – and more and more young Spaniards are using *"el Messenger"* to communicate with their friends.

Mi ordenador está afectado por un virus – My computer has a virus

Pinchar en un enlace – To click on a link

Hacer doble clic – To double-click

Email en cadena – Chain email

Las páginas web, correo y comercio electrónico –
Web pages, email and ecommerce

Bajar un archivo de Internet – To download a file
from Internet

Se aconseja utilizar accesos seguros – You are
advised to use secure sites

Tener el anti-virus al día – Keep your anti-virus updated

Actualizar, editar, atrás, adelante, imprimir –
Refresh (update), edit, back, forwards, print

Menú, detener, ventana, ayuda – Menu, stop,
window, help

No tengo acceso a Internet – I haven't got Internet
access

Soy un desastre para la tecnología – I am hopeless
when it comes to technology

"Nothing to do with carnival!
I've just come out of the closet!"

FIESTAS

Carnival time

Carnival, dating back to pagan times when probably it celebrated the arrival of spring, has been popular in Spain for centuries, though it was banned by the Inquisition and more recently by the dictator Primo de Rivera... It got going again with the restoration of democracy.

Like other fiestas in Spain, *Carnaval* is a time for merry-making and especially the singing of satirical songs poking fun at celebrities and politicians and the topics of the day.

It is the last big fling before Lent.

Cadiz is considered to have the best, biggest and loudest carnival, lasting for ten riotous days in February. Troupes of musicians known as *Chirigotas* and *Comparsas* roam the streets in fantastic costumes for days on end, beating drums and singing their irreverent songs.

Carnaval – Carnival

Pregón – A proclamation read out to inaugurate the festivities

Pregonero – The person who reads the proclamation

Dios Momo – The god who rules over Carnival

Comparsas/Chirigotas/Murgas – Troubadours who sing satirical songs

Disfraz – Disguise, fancy dress

Disfrazado – In disguise

Domingo de Piñata – First Sunday of Lent

Piñata – A box or other container full of sweets and toys

Concurso – Contest

Todos los niños van disfrazados – All the children go in fancy dress

Incluso los más pequeños – Even the smallest of them

La cabalgata es el sábado por la tarde – The parade is on Saturday afternoon

Y los fuegos artificiales por la noche – And the fireworks at night

Las carrozas son muy divertidas – The floats are very amusing

Se cantan comparsas y chirigotas – People sing satirical songs lampooning celebrities and politicians

Cádiz es famoso por su Carnaval – Cadiz is famous for its Carnival

El de Estepona es muy entrañable – The one in Estepona is very endearing

Todo el pueblo participa – The whole town takes part

¿Por qué se entierra una sardina al final? – Why does a sardine get buried at the end?

Y en Malaga, ¿por qué es un boquerón? – And why is it an anchovy in Malaga?

¿Y un mollete en Antequera? – And a bap in Antequera?

¿A qué hora sale la comitiva? – What times does the procession leave?

No sé, pero deben verla, es muy divertida – I don't know but you should see it, it is very funny

Todos van llorando – Everyone cries

All the fun of the fair

An article in a British newspaper recently referred to Malaga's *feria* as the biggest street party in Europe, and urged its readers not to rush straight from the airport to the beaches to the east and west, but to stay in the city and enjoy all the fun of the fair.

It could have added that the Malaga fair is not only the biggest, spreading geographically throughout the city centre, bullring district, and a vast area on the outskirts where the fairground proper is installed, but also the longest. It lasts for ten long, hot, fun-filled days and nights

Little work gets done during the *feria* – and it's pointless trying to phone anyone. They will either be sleeping it off or they have already left the house to join in the daytime festivities. These start around midday in the city centre with dancing and singing in the streets, moving on to the bullring in the

"No Sevillanas this year Paula. We have to sing Endesas"... (to celebrate the electicity company Sevillana changing its name to Endesa).

early evening and then to the fairground at night, where the carousing goes on until the early hours.

Malagueños are rightfully proud of their *feria* and are eager to point out to you that, unlike their rival in Seville, the *casetas* at the Malaga fair are open to everyone, the only restriction being when they are just too full to hold another partygoer.

Las casetas están llenas de farolillos – The entertainment areas are full of paper lanterns

Y normalmente tienen un escenario y un bar – And usually they have a stage and a bar

Y una pista de baile – And a dance floor

Las calles se cubren con toldos – The streets are covered with awnings

La gente se refresca con cerveza y fino – People refresh themselves with beer or dry sherry

Los caballos se pasean en el Real – Horses are ridden around the fairground

Lo mejor son los trajes típicos regionales – Really eye-catching are the regional costumes

Y los trajes de faralaes de las mujeres – And the gypsy dresses of the women

Se bailan muchas sevillanas – *"Sevillanas"* are danced a lot

Pero los verdiales son el baile de Malaga – But the *"verdiales"* is the typical Malaga dance

En muchas casetas te invitan a comer – You are invited to eat in many casetas

Quieren demostrar lo hospitalario que son los malagueños – They want to show you how hospitable the *malagueños* are

Las casetas de las peñas ofrecen platos típicos – The clubs' *casetas* offer typical dishes

Por la tarde vamos a los toros – This evening we are going to the bullfight

Hay conciertos gratuitos en la caseta municipal – There are free concerts in the municipal *caseta*

Terminas la semana de feria totalmente agotado/a – You end the feria week totally exhausted

A mi me gusta más la feria de día – I prefer the daytime fair

Y la feria taurina – And the bullfighting fair

Tengo un abono, en la sombra – I have a season ticket, for the shady side of the bullring

Los bares cierran a las nueve en feria – The bars close at 9 during the fair

¿Te vas a vestir esta noche? – Are you going to dress up tonight?

Sí, mi mujer va vestida de flamenca – Yes, my wife is going in her flamenco dress

Y yo con traje corto – And I am wearing my flamenco suit

Feasting at Christmas

The most festive meal of a Spanish Christmas is the one served on the evening of the 24th, when all the family sit down to a gigantic feast, traditionally of fish and seafood, though some families will opt for a special meat dish and fill the table with plates of appetizing slices of cheese, ham, sausages and other delicacies.

The midday meal on Christmas day is again an occasion for family gatherings and another feast. Never absent from these festive occasions are the plates upon plates of those delicious individually-wrapped Christmas cakes – the almond-tasting *mantecados* and *polvorones*. Another all-time favourite is *turrón*, a kind of nougat, that comes in more textures and flavours with each Christmas.

It's not only on the Christmas table you will see these tasty treats. They are handed around right throughout the festive season, and in shops and business establishments you will see them piled high in a tray alongside a bottle of *anís* or coñac, or both, for the customers to help themselves.

Pavo/salmón/cordero/solomillo/cochinillo – Turkey, salmon, lamb, fillet steak/suckling pig

Pavo relleno/pato a la naranja – Stuffed turkey, duck *à l'orange*

Nueces/castañas/pistachos – Walnuts/chestnuts/ pistachios

El marisco es muy caro en Navidad – Seafood is very expensive at Christmas

Muchos dulces navideños se hacen en Estepa – Many Christmas sweets are made in Estepa

Polvorón/Mantecado – wrapped almond-based Spanish Christmas cakes

Turrón – Nougat-type sweet made with almonds and honey

Peladillas – Sugared almonds

Aumenta el consumo de cava – Consumption of *cava* (Spanish champagne) goes up

El día veinticinco es festivo – The 25th is a public holiday

Sing a song at Christmas

When people talk about Christmas carols in English, we think not only of the "Holly and the Ivy" type of seasonal song, but also the "Once in royal David's City" variety at church carol services. In Spain, the word usually used for "carol" is *villancico*, but this originally meant a peasant or village song, sung at country festivals marking important dates in rural life.

So it is hardly surprising that if you ask a Spaniard to sing a *villancico*, the chances are that you will be treated to a rendering of the children's favourite *Peces en el Río* ("Fishes in the River") and not the imported *Noche de paz, noche de amor.* ("Silent Night").

Villancicos are most unlikely to be accompanied by an organ. Dating back to the 15th and 16th centuries, they are usually accompanied by more rowdy and primitive instruments, such as *zambombas* (a drum shaped artefact with rabbit skin stretched over the top and a *caña* [reed] to pump up and down producing a very distinctive and rather rude noise), and *panderetas* (tambourines), which can be bought at the Christmas fairs right up until the arrival of the Three Kings on January 6th.

Many Spaniards claim to have learned a lot of English by singing the songs of the Beatles in their youth. Learning Spanish might well be made easier and more fun by singing with the children "Fishes in the River" – or at least join in the chorus:

"Pero mira como beben los peces en el río
Pero mira como beben por ver a Dios nacido
Beben y beben y vuelven a beber
Los peces en el río por ver a Dios nacer."

"But look how the fish drink in the river
But look how they drink upon seeing the newborn God
They drink and drink and drink again
The fishes in the river, upon seeing the newborn God."

Un villancico popular – A popular carol

El Niño/la Virgen María/San José – The (Christ) Child/the Virgin Mary/St Joseph

Los Magos de Oriente – The Wise Men from the East

Los pastores/el buey – The shepherds/the ox

La estrella/el portal/el pesebre/la cuna – The star/the stable/the manger/the cradle

Los niños van de puerta en puerta cantando – Children go from door to door singing

Se les regala turrón o dulces – They are given *"turrón"* or sweets

Party time

Christmas is over but the biggest party of the year is yet to come. Spaniards see in the New Year by gulping down 12 grapes or *uvas de la suerte*, one on each stroke of midnight. Many of them enjoy this ritual in the town square.

Then the celebration begins and the carousing goes on until dawn, when those merrymakers who are still awake and sober enough crowd into the bars to enjoy the traditional hot chocolate and *churros*.

Las uvas de la suerte – The twelve lucky grapes

Las campanadas de las doce – The twelve strokes of midnight

Feliz Año Nuevo – Happy New Year

Paz y Prosperidad – Peace and Prosperity

Salud y Suerte – Good Health and Good Fortune

A ti y a los tuyos – To you and yours

Desayunaremos chocolate con churros – We will have hot chocolate and *"churros"* for breakfast

El día uno es festivo – January 1st is a holiday

The Three Wise Men

Anybody who thinks that Spanish traditions are dying out, only need to go for a walk on January 6th and see children wobbling around on new bikes, girls pushing doll's prams and boys manipulating their remote control toy cars, to know that the *Reyes* (the Kings) or the Wise Men from the East are still making their annual trip to every Spanish town and *pueblo*.

The previous night, vast numbers of children would have gone with their parents to see the Three Kings parade through the streets, accompanied by a wide variety of floats. You might wonder what an exotic belly-dancer or a Walt Disney figure is doing in the cavalcade, but as long as they and their attendants threw enough sweets into the crowds, nobody asks.

After Gaspar, Melchior and Balthasar have delivered their gifts to every household, they vanish until next year, but the festivities continue. Traditionally, January 6th is a day for family visiting, picking up gifts from all the relatives, and enjoying a last celebratory meal.

One member of the family will be king or queen for the day, after finding a lucky charm in a portion of the traditional ring-shaped *Roscón de Reyes* cake. Then the children play with their new toys before it's time for bed, and next day it's back to school.

"The Three Kings brought me a doll which walks, puts on make-up, talks, dances, cooks, washes up, puts the washing machine on and irons"... "Where is it?"... " Gone to live with dad."

La Cabalgata de Reyes – The parade of the three kings

Esta noche vienen los Reyes – The kings are coming tonight

¿Qué te van a traer los Reyes? – What are they going to bring you?

¿Qué les has pedido? – What have you asked them for?

Pero, ¿te has portado bien este año? – But have you been good this year?

Si no, te traerán carbón – If not, they will bring you (a lump of) coal

Los mayores también reciben regalos – Adults (the older people) get gifts too

Los niños piden juguetes – The children ask for toys

Este año, muchos ordenadores y cámaras digitales – This year, lots of computers and digital cameras

Un paje tira caramelos desde la carroza – A page throws sweets from the float

Los niños cogen kilos de caramelos – The children collect kilos of sweets

"Wet weather continues throughout the peninsula."

THE WEATHER

¡Qué Calor!

For most of the year along the Mediterranean Coast, especially in the south, the weather is not usually a hot topic of conversation. There's not much you can say about a fierce sun beating down from a cloudless blue sky for months on end, except perhaps *"¡qué calor!"* and "do you have air conditioning?"

We can, of course, comment countless times on how lucky we are to be cooled at night by a refreshing sea breeze while the poor devils in landlocked cities such as Seville and Cordoba are sweating it out all through the day and night.

Weather talk tends to pick up a bit during the winter months, though, when sunny days are broken up by storms and cold spells and we can even get glimpses of the snow on the distant *sierras*. Then we can nod wisely and say things like "this winter sunshine is fine for the tourists but we need rain for the *campo*." Or, after a week-long downpour, "we need a lot more rain to fill the *pantanos* else there will be no water next summer." Or "this rain is too heavy; it will flatten the crops and run out to sea."

Then there is all the excitement after a storm when we can talk for hours about the flash floods in town and enjoy romantic conversations by candlelight during the power cuts. It doesn't last long, though. Before we know it, the sun is beating down again from a cloudless blue sky for months on end and, once again, all we can say about the weather is *"¡qué calor!"*

¡Qué calor! ¿Verdad? – Hot, isn't it?

Menos mal que tenemos aire acondicionado – Just as well we have air conditioning

¿Cuándo tienes tú las vacaciones? – When are you taking your holiday?

En octubre, cuando haga menos calor – In October, when it's not so hot

En agosto no se puede ni ir a la playa – In August you can't even go to the beach

Bueno, en el interior hace más calor – Well, it's hotter inland

En Granada están a cuarenta grados – In Granada it's 40°

Hace calor hasta en Navidad - It is hot even at Christmas

Aquí por lo menos refresca el mar – Here at least the sea breeze makes it cooler

El clima es muy benigno – The weather is very mild

Y las temperaturas suaves – And the temperatures are mild

La predicción del tiempo – The weather forecast

El cielo está nublado – It is cloudy (the sky is clouded)

Cuando llueve, todo el mundo coge el coche – When it rains, everyone goes by car

En cuanto caen cuatro gotas – As soon as it starts to rain

Hace viento – It is windy

Se verán claros salpicados de nubes – Clear skies with the occasional cloud

Ligera bajada de temperatura – Slight drop in temperature

Cielos cubiertos – Overcast skies

Por la tarde, algunos chubascos – Scattered showers in the afternoon

Están cayendo chuzos de punta – It is raining cats and dogs (pointed pikes)

Ya ha entrado el invierno – Winter has arrived

Hace frío en el interior – It is cold inland

Hace un frío que pela – It is freezing cold

Granizo del tamaño de una pelota de tenis – Hail stones as big as tennis balls

Escarcha – Frost

Estoy helado/a – I am frozen

¿Dónde puedo comprar leña y pastilles para encender la chimenea? – Where can I buy wood and firelighters?

¿Has puesto la manta eléctrica? – Have you put the electric blanket on?

Hace más frio que en Rusia – It's colder than in Russia

Tenemos la calefacción averiada – Our heating isn't working

¡Qué frío! – How cold it is!

Hay nieve en las carreteras – There is snow on the roads

Hay hielo en las carreteras – There is ice on the roads

Las carreteras están cortadas – The roads are blocked (closed)

Hay pueblos enteros aislados por la nieve – Whole villages are snowed in

En Malaga nunca nieva – It never snows in Malaga

Pronto hará de nuevo calor – It will soon be warm again

"The coach says it's time to go out on the field, you've been warming up long enough."

SPORTS AND LEISURE

Football talk

When it comes to being understood in Spanish, people who talk sports have a definite advantage.

English golfers will feel at home when they hear the words *el buggy, el green* or *el rough* used on a Spanish golf course, and tennis buffs will have no problem following the score at a Spanish match, though "love" is referred to as cero.

It's even easier when it comes to football. Never mind that language purists insist the game is called *balonpié*; the Spanish fan next to you at the game will perfectly understand your enthusiasm for *fútbol,* and it should be no problem to yell "corner", "penalti" or "*igol!*" in unison.

Marca, the sports daily, is the most widely read newspaper in Spain, selling more than half a million copies, and football is by far the most popular sport. Our home team Malaga draws crowds of supporters and possibly has more foreigners amongst its fans than any other Spanish club. Indeed, going to a football match must be one of the easiest ways to integrate with Spaniards without actually knowing much Spanish.

Malaga juega en Primera – Malaga play in the top division

La Copa del Rey – The King's Cup (Spain's version of the F.A. Cup)

La selección nacional – The national team

Representa a España – He plays for Spain

El fútbol es el rey de los deportes – Football is the king of sports

La afición/el entrenador – The fans/the manager

Ha sido un empate – It was a draw

Ganaron dos a cero – They won 2-0

Perdieron en casa – They lost at home

La semana que viene juegan fuera – Next week they play away

El árbitro/los jugadores/el portero – The referee/ the players/the goalkeeper

¡Falta!/ ¡Fuera! – Foul!/Send him off!

Nos vemos en la taquilla – We'll meet at the ticket office

Están en los vestuarios – They are in the dressing rooms

Prórroga/descanso – Extra time/half time

Los _"hooligans"_ – Often used interchangeably with "English fans"

Tarjeta amarilla/roja – Yellow/red card

Saque/saque de esquina/saque de banda – Kick off/corner kick/throw-in

Tengo abono – I have a season ticket

La temporada empieza el domingo – The season starts on Sunday

¿Vas al partido? – Are you going to the match?

No, lo veré en televisión – No I'll watch it on TV

Sports for everyone

The climate in southern Spain of course is ideal for sports and you can enjoy, practically throughout the year, just about every outdoor activity in the alphabet, from athletics to tennis. Golf is big along the *Costas*, and so are water sports, especially in summer, and in winter the snow slopes are close by.

Sports facilities have improved enormously during the past few years and are attracting top sports people from all over Europe, who come to the sun to train in the winter. For example, Torremolinos on the Costa del Sol has an Olympic size swimming pool where champions train and is planning to build a second one.

¿Practicas algún deporte? – Do you take part in any sports?

Soy jugador de fútbol/tenis – I am a football/tennis player

Lo mío es la natación – I'm into swimming

Una vez por semana hago largos – I swim lengths once a week

¿Sabes montar a caballo? – Can you ride?

Prefiero los deportes acuáticos – I prefer water sports

Me encanta el baloncesto – I love basketball

Los españoles destacan en el golf y tenis – Spain has outstanding golf and tennis players

Hay nieve en las pistas, podemos ir a esquiar – There is snow on the slopes, we can go skiing

Nos vemos en el hoyo diecinueve – See you on the 19th (hole)

At the gym

Keeping fit could hardly be easier in southern Spain. Besides all the excellent sports facilities and workout centres, there is an almost constant supply of good weather, offering no excuse for not going out for a jog or cycling to work.

Even so, few people seem to work out, except perhaps in the new year period when they say they need to burn off all the *turrón* they ate at Christmas, and around May when thoughts turn to last year's bikini and this year's white flab. Then the gyms see a rush of new members, which falls off sharply when summer proper arrives.

Es importante calentar primero – It is important to warm up first

Después hacemos unas tablas – Then we'll do a series of floor exercises

El clima en la Costa invita a hacer footing – The Coast weather encourages you to go jogging

La natación es muy recomendable para la salud – Swimming is very good for your health

Y también la danza – And so is dancing

El gimnasio/la gimnasia/los gimnastas – The gymnasium, gymnastics, the gymnasts

Aumentar la resistencia y quemar calorías – To increase stamina and burn calories

Quisiera asistir a clases de aerobic – I'd like to attend aerobic classes

El ejercicio ayuda a estar en forma y sentirse a gusto – Exercise helps you keep fit and feel good

Apuntarse a clases de step – Put your name down for some stepping classes

No tengo voluntad para ir todos los días – I don't have the willpower to go every day

Hacer karate/pesas/ boxeo/ lucha libre – To do karate, weight- lifting, boxing, wrestling.

Se aburre haciendo gimnasia solo/sola – He/she gets bored doing gymnastics alone

Me gustaría tener un entrenador personal – I'd like to have a personal trainer

At the beach

You can do almost everything you want on a Spanish beach, and prohibition signs are kept to a minimum. You can play ball, fly a kite, go topless, listen to music and even put up a tent and cook a *paella*. In summer at weekends, large Spanish families arrive early at the beach with just about everything bar the kitchen sink.

Among the few restrictions in force that are generally respected are the red flags, indicating that it is dangerous to go into the sea, and the signs prohibiting dogs on the beach, though this one is relaxed somewhat in winter when there are few people on the beach, and of course the "No ball games" sign on crowded beaches is routinely ignored unless the more passive bathers start getting irate.

Whatever anyone tries to tell you to the contrary, any "Private beach" signs can safely be ignored, as they are illegal. Spain's beaches are public and although certain establishments will do their best to indicate otherwise, public access has to be provided.

For goodness sake, Paqui! Where have you put the keys to the bathroom?"

¿Cogemos unas tumbonas? – Shall we hire some sunbeds?

¿Es peligroso bañarse aquí? – Is it dangerous to bathe here?

Las mujeres van topless en la Costa – Women go topless along the Costa del Sol

Se prohiben los perros y los caballos – Dogs and horses not allowed

Vamos a alquilar un hidropedal – We are going to hire a pedalo

¿Cuánto cuesta la hora? – How much does it cost per hour?

Me gusta hacer pesca submarina – I like going underwater fishing

Zona reservada para barcos de recreo – Area reserved for boats

Hacer castillos de arena – To build sandcastles

Comer en un chiringuito – To eat in a beach bar

Tomar el sol – To sunbathe

Tirarse de cabeza – To dive

Crema solar, factor veinte – Sun cream, protection factor twenty

Tostarse al sol – To tan (literally, to toast oneself)

Quiero ponerme morena – I want to get a tan

Pero sólo consigo quemarme – But I only (manage to) get burned

¿Tienes libro/toalla/gorro/gafas de sol? – Have you got your book/towel/cap/your sunglasses?

Los flotadores/la pelota/el cubo y la pala – Water wings/ball/bucket and spade

Dinero para refrescos y helados – And money for cold drinks and ice cream

Y para el hidropedal, las tumbonas, y la sombrilla – And for the paddle boat, sunbeds and sunshade

La nevera con los bocadillos y la cerveza – The cool box with the sandwiches and beer

Se me ha olvidado el sacacorchos – I have forgotten the corkscrew

Un traje de neopreno – A wetsuit

Aletas/tubo y gafas de buceo – Flippers/ snorkel and mask

YOUR HOME

Buying a home

Buying a home anywhere is a huge undertaking but in a foreign country, and in a language you don't speak, it can be fraught with potential hazards. The laws and procedures are different here and you really need an expert to steer you safely through the paperwork.

It's easy while under the influence of sun, wine and the holiday spirit to throw caution to the wind and believe everything you are told by the jolly nice chap you meet in a bar who just happens to know where you can find your dream home – or be taken in when the real estate agent says he's a lawyer too and can handle everything for you.

Just as at home, not everyone will tell you the truth, so if the vendor tells you the property is very quiet and gets the early morning sun, go for another look on Friday night and Saturday morning.

Piso a estrenar, aparcamiento opcional – A new flat, with option to buy a parking/garage space

Apartamento tres dormitorios, cocina amue-blada – Three bedroomed apartment, furnished kitchen

Particular. Chalet pareado, jardín particular – Private sale. Semi-detached villa, private garden

Soleado, tranquilo, luminoso. Amplio salón – Sunny, quiet, light. Large sitting room

Doy facilidades – Terms negotiable

Busco un chalet con vistas al mar – I am looking for a villa with sea views

Con piscina, trastero y suelos de mármol – With a pool, junk room and marble floors

Armarios empotrados, ascensor y azotea – Built-in wardrobes, lift and rooftop terrace

Televisión por satélite – satellite TV

Parabólica – satellite dish (for the development)

Puerta blindada, doble acristalamiento – Reinforced (security) door, double glazing

Magnífica inversión, reformadísima – wonderful investment, supermodernised

Urge traslado – owner relocating so fast sale

Calefacción central, aire acondicionado – central heating, air conditioning

¿Quieren ver el piso piloto? – would you like to see the show flat?

Entrada – Hallway. Also a down payment

Último piso, Ático – Top floor flat, penthouse

No he conseguido una hipoteca – I haven't been able to get a mortgage

¿Tiene algo para alquilar? – Do you have anything to rent?

Communities of property owners

Most property complexes operate on a community system whereby all the owners belong to a *Comunidad de Propietarios* and have a say in the running of communal facilities such as lifts, swimming pools, gardens, etc. Every owner has a vote but, depending on the size of the property, some may hold more sway than others.

The community is governed by statutes and has a president, who is elected each year. This post is so little coveted in some communities that "volunteers" are found by picking a name out of a hat. A general meeting is held at least once a year. Warning must be given well in advance, and if you can't attend personally you can appoint a proxy. Otherwise, you will just have to abide by the decisions made by those who do attend.

A monthly charge is made to each owner to cover maintenance costs and this varies according to the services supplied and the amenities available. In a small block of apartments with no lift the fees can be negligible, but the monthly fee can be hefty in a luxury development with swimming pool, porter, cleaners and gardeners

Comunidad de Propietarios – Community of property owners

Cuota – Fees

Recibo – Receipt

Presidente, secretario – President, Secretary

Tesorero – Treasurer

Administrador de fincas – Property Administrator

Estatutos – Statutes or by-laws

Poder – Proxy

Votar a favor – To vote in favour

Votar en contra – To vote against

Quejarse – To complain

Libro de Actas – Minute book

Póliza de seguro – Insurance policy

Gastos – Expenses

Orden del día – Agenda

Home reforms

Having lived in Spain for most of my adult life, I know a thing or two about home reforms in this country. I know, for example, that they can start as soon as you move into a brand-new home and find that the light switches and electric plugs are in hard-to-reach places.

When you decide to do a big reform that involves removing a wall or two and you want to avoid bashing into water pipes and electricity cables, you start looking for the house plan and then remember you were never given one. It really doesn't matter because the plans seldom match exactly the finished building. The plumber and the electrician had their own ideas about where the pipes and cables should go.

The work takes much longer than expected and spreads itself into every corner of the house, so you have to move out while it's being done. When you get back you find that the plug for the fridge has mysteriously moved itself to a spot right behind the dishwasher.

Esta casa está muy deteriorada – This house is very delapidated

El techo se está cayendo – The ceiling (also roof) is falling down

Un suelo blanco no es nada práctico – A white floor is not at all practical

Vamos a hacer reformas – We are going to renovate

Queremos tirar este tabique y hacer el salón más grande – We want to pull this wall down and make the sitting room bigger

También ampliaremos el cuarto de baño – We'll also extend the bathroom

Decorar la salita, mejorar la ventilación – Decorate the (little) living room, improve the ventilation

Abrir otra ventana, instalar calefacción central – Put in another window, install central heating

Tenemos ya aire acondicionado – We already have air conditioning

No necesito decorador, lo haré yo – I don't need a decorator, I'll do it

Hay muchas tiendas de bricolaje – There are lots of DIY shops

Quiero renovar la cocina entera – I want a completely new kitchen

Y cambiar el papel pintado por azulejos – And to change the wallpaper for tiles

Un suelo de madera en vez de moqueta – A wooden floor instead of carpet

El electricista viene mañana – The electrician is coming tomorrow

El fontanero ha prometido estar aquí también – The plumber has promised to be here too

Hoy me traen los electrodomésticos – They are bringing the white goods today

Pero el suelo está levantado todavía – But the floor is still up

No tenemos ni agua ni electricidad – We have no water or electricity

La casa está llena de escombros – The house is full of rubble

Haz las maletas, nos vamos a un hotel – Pack the bags, we are going to a hotel

"Can I give you a lift?"...
"No thanks we're in a hurry."

ON THE ROAD

Coping with an accident

Dealing with a traffic accident in Spain is really no different from dealing with one anywhere else, except perhaps in the reactions of the drivers concerned. Road rage is unlikely, but occasionally emotions run high in the form of much shouting and arm waving, which is how Spaniards tend to relieve their feelings. In one recent accident involving five cars, the only injury sustained was a stubbed toe – caused when one of the drivers, after seeing the damage to his car, kicked a nearby cement post.

Make sure you have all the necessary documents in the car, including some form of identification, your driving licence, insurance papers (with a receipt showing the policy is paid up-to-date), and the plastic card the insurance company usually gives you with the phone number of a 24-hour road service.

When in an accident, always be polite and stay calm and, if the police are not present to take down the details, make sure you take the name, car number and insurance details of the other driver. And don't forget to put on your obligatory reflective jacket when you get out of the car – and put out the triangular warning sign at the regulated distance behind your car while you're sorting things out.

Por favor enséñeme su documentación – Show me your documents, please

El carnet de conducir y el seguro – Driving licence and insurance

¿El coche está a su nombre? – Is the car in your name?

No, es de la empresa – No, it is a company car

El último recibo – The last receipt

¿Como ocurrió el accidente? – How did the accident happen

¿Hay alguien herido? – Is anyone injured?

La ambulancia está de camino – The ambulance is on its way

Voy a necesitar una grúa – I am going to need a tow truck

No llevo el carnet – I haven't got my driving licence with me

El seguro no me ha llegado, está en el correo – The insurance hasn't arrived, it is in the post

Me robaron el pasaporte la semana pasada –
My passport was stolen last week

Estoy muy nervioso, no sé ni donde vivo –
I am very nervous, I don't even know where I live

Mi apellido es Wright. ¿Se lo deletreo? –
My surname is Wright. Shall I spell it for you?

No ha sido culpa mia – It wasn't my fault

El que iba delante mío frenó bruscamente –
The one in front of me braked suddenly

En España se conduce por la derecha – In Spain
one drives on the right

**El límite de velocidad en autopista es de ciento
veinte kilometros por hora –** The speed limit on
motorways is 120 kph

Cinco millas equivale a ocho kilómetros – Five
miles equal eight kilometres

Autopista de peaje – Toll motorway

El tráfico hoy ha sido peor que nunca – The traffic
today was worse than ever

Había colas hasta en el acceso a la autovía –
There were queues even on the slip road to the dual
carriageway

Y un atasco en el semáforo - And a traffic jam at
the traffic lights

He tardado cuarenta minutos en llegar - It took
me 40 minutes to get here

**Se circula bien cuando los colegios están de
vacaciones –** Driving is fine when the schools are on
holiday

La curva de La Cala es un punto negro – The
bend at La Cala is a black spot

La hora punta – Rush hour

Ceda el paso – Give way

Carretera cortada – Road closed

Prohibido el paso – No entry

Cambio de sentido – Change of direction

¡El semáforo estaba en rojo! – The traffic lights were red!

Yo tenía prioridad, salía por su derecha – I had the right of way, I was coming from your right

No se puede adelantar por la derecha – You can't overtake on the right

Ha saltado el "stop" – You went through a Stop sign

Es ilegal usar el móvil con el coche en marcha – It's illegal to use a mobile phone while driving

¿Dónde está la gasolinera más cercana? – Where is the nearest petrol station?

¿Me llena el tanque, por favor? – Would you fill up (my tank) please?

Gasolina super/gasolina sin plomo/gasoil/diesel – 4-star petrol, unleaded petrol, diesel

Your car and the police

Penalties for drunken driving are quite stiff now in Spain. It was once possible to drink all you wanted to and know you were not going to be breathalysed on the way home. These days, there's a good chance you are going to be stopped and, if you are over the top, you can lose your driving licence for a year.

In my area the breathalysing controls seem to be rather predictable in their movements. At a late-night party recently, I was told by my hosts the exact time and under which bridge I would most likely be stopped, and sure enough there they were, pulling cars over and putting drivers through the

"Quick, Lola, there's a parking space free in Calle Larios."

breathalyser test. I was sober, of course!

Every year, the list of traffic regulations seems to get longer and the fines for all manner of violations, from speeding to not wearing a safety belt, get higher. And visitors should take note: the police can demand payment on the spot from non-residents.

Control de alcoholemia – Breathalyser test

Negarse a soplar – Refuse to blow into the bag

Análisis de sangre – Blood test

Control de velocidad – Speed trap

Aparque el coche aquí a la derecha por favor – Park here on the right, please

¿Quiere abrir el maletero? – Would you mind opening the boot?

¿Me enseña su carnet de conducir? – Show me your driving licence please

¿Lleva bombillas de repuesto? – Are you carrying spare light bulbs?

No le funciona la luz de freno – Your brake lights aren't working

No llevaba el cinturón de seguridad – You weren't wearing your seat belt

Le tengo que multar – I'm going to have to fine you

Bueno, me ha pillado – It's a fair cop

Llamamos grúa – We'll call for the tow truck (if you park here)

Aparcar en doble fila – Double parking

Un coche, un turismo – A car, a passenger car

Un deportivo, una furgoneta, un camión – A sports car, a van, a lorry

Un coche automático – An automatic

Un todo terreno – A four wheel drive

El cambio de marcha – The gear stick

El capó, la carrocería, las ruedas – The bonnet, the bodywork, the wheels

Los neumáticos, el limpiaparabrisas, el volante – The tyres, the windscreen wiper, the steering wheel

El parachoque delantero – The front bumper

El embrague, el amortiguador – The clutch, the shock absorber

El depósito del líquido de freno – The brake fluid reservoir

El espejo retrovisor, el asiento trasero – The rear view mirror, the back seat

GETTING AROUND

Asking the way

Asking for directions to your hotel or the train station can be fraught with peril in any country but even more so in Spain, where the locals are so anxious to be helpful that they will confidently give you exact instructions on where you want to go even if they haven't the faintest idea of how to get there.

For instance, you stop your car in Granada and ask the way to the Alhambra and the person you ask for directions is a non-driver who has just arrived by train from Santander. He won't say so, though. He tells you to turn round, go back about 200 metres, take the first left and then the first right.

A passer-by, who has stopped to listen, disagrees and they flag down a car going in the other direction to ask the driver's opinion. A small crowd gathers and the traffic piles up – until you finally lose your nerve and say *muchas gracias* and drive on.

Next time make sure you ask a taxi driver. He surely knows the way – and may even speak some English.

Perdone, ¿me puede decir dónde está Correos? – Excuse me, can you direct me to the Post Office?

¿Dónde está la estación de autobuses/Renfe? – Where is the bus/railway station?

¿Por dónde se va a Motril? – Which way to Motril?

Todo seguido – Straight ahead

Todo recto hasta el semáforo – Carry on as far as the traffic lights

A la derecha – On the right

A la izquierda – On the left

Gire a la derecha – Turn right

Gire a la izquierda – Turn left

La segunda bocacalle a la izquierda – The second turning on the left

Después del puente – After the bridge

Dé media vuelta – Turn round

Siga Vd. por aquí – Carry on this way

Siga Vd. trescientos metros – Carry on for 300 metres

Tres manzanas – Three blocks

Enfrente de la iglesia – Opposite the church

Delante del banco – In front of the bank

Detrás del cine – Behind the cinema

La carretera da un rodeo hacia la izquierda – The road bears to the left

Siga las señales a... – Follow the signs to...

Taxis

Taking a taxi is often the best way to get around town. It's not expensive and taxi drivers usually know how to avoid heavy traffic. And what bliss, at the end of a shopping spree, to fall into the nearest taxi with your bundles or boxes and bags and be dropped off at your doorstep.

Spanish taxi drivers are talkative and a mine of information and many of them in the tourist areas speak a little English. On many occasions they have filled me in on the grisly details of a murder, explained why an ambitious city project will never get off the ground, or warned me which streets an unaccompanied female would do better to avoid.

It is quite easy just to walk out and catch a taxi in the street, or head for the nearest taxi rank, but the radio taxi service is a boon at peak times or for going to the airport at the crack of dawn. Don't be put off by the thought of explaining your requirements in Spanish. All you need to say is where you are and they will give you the taxi's number and tell you how long it will take to reach you.

¿Me manda un taxi a... – Would you send a taxi to...?

¿Me lleva al aeropuerto? – Would you take me to the airport?

Calle Larios, por favor – Larios street, please

¿A qué altura? – How far down?

A la altura de Correos – By the Post Office

Aquí mismo – Right here

¿Cuanto tardará? – How long will it take?

¿Podría ir más deprisa? – Could you go a bit faster?

Llevo prisa – I'm in a bit of a hurry.

¿Le importaría ir más despacio? – Do you mind going slower?

¿Cuánto es la tarifa de aquí al centro? – How much from here to the centre?

¿Qué sobrecargo hay por la maleta? – How much extra do you charge per suitcase?

¿Podría esperar un momento? – Would you wait a moment?

¿Me da Vd. su número de licencia? – Would you give me your licence number?

¿Podría bajar la música? – Do you mind turning the music down?

¿Está permitido fumar? – May I smoke?

Local buses and trains

If you are a tourist, it can be fun just getting on a local bus and seeing where it takes you. Visitors to Granada, for example, should make a point of riding on the mini-buses which set out from the *Plaza Nueva* and for less than one euro take you up to the Alhambra or the Sacromonte caves or round the narrow streets of the Albaicín.

If you are using the local bus service to get from a to b, you can usually get a discount by buying a card of ten tickets from a ticket dispenser, and you should ask about discounts for students and pensioners. If you don't have time to buy a ticket in the bus station you can always pay the driver on the bus, which isn't always the case with trains. If you don't buy your ticket before getting on the Costa del Sol coastal train, for example, it could cost you double.

¿De dónde sale el autobús? – Where does the bus leave from?

Hay una parada al final de esta calle – There is a stop at the end of this street

¿Todos los autobuses van al centro? – Do all the buses go to the centre?

Tiene que coger el once o el diecisiete – You need to get a number 11 or a 17

¿Me puede avisar cuando lleguemos al museo? – Can you let me know when we get to the museum?

Me bajo en la próxima (parada) – I am getting off at the next stop

Los autobuses de recorrido largo salen de la estación de autobuses – The long distance buses leave from the bus station

¿Me da un billete de ida y vuelta, a Sevilla? – Can I have a return ticket to Seville?

Los autocares son modernos, con aire acondicionado – The coaches are modern, with air conditioning

Hacen una parada de descanso a mitad camino – They make a rest stop, half way

El autobús pasa cada diez minutos - The bus passes every ten minutes

A veces pasan tres seguidos. Si están llenos, no paran – Sometimes three go by together. If they are full they don't stop

"Before we prepared our tax returns we were planning a lovely Caribbean trip with the children"... "And now?"... "We'll be bathing off the Huelin beach in Malaga."

TRAVEL

At the hotel

One of the first hotels to open its doors in pioneering Torremolinos on the Costa del Sol was the Hotel Montemar, which began operating as a parador in 1933 with seven bedrooms. Most of the first guests of course were English. Then came the Hotel Roca in 1942, where full board set you back 32 pesetas (€0.19) per day, and a "special" dinner was a mere 27 pesetas (€0.16)!

Then came the tourist boom in the sixties which transformed the town, and the boom grew bigger and bigger until today there are countless hotels all along the *Costas*, offering every kind of accommodation from cheap *pensiones* to five-star hotels pampering clients with every kind of luxury.

Long gone are the days when foreign couples arriving at their hotel were ask to show their "family book" to prove they were married, and inland farm workers flocked to the coast to find work in the hotels and, no doubt, to chat up the foreign girls on the beach, who were referred to as *suecas*, Swedish girls, regardless of their nationality. These days, hotel staff are fully trained in special schools and enjoy a good reputation for professionalism.

¿Dónde hay un buen hotel? – Where is there a good hotel?

¿Es muy caro? – is it very expensive?

¿Tiene una habitación para una sola persona? – Have you got a single room?

Una habitación doble – A double room

Con cama de matrimonio – With a double bed

Con dos camas – With two beds

¿Pueden poner una cama supletoria para el niño? – Can you provide an extra bed for a child?

¿Está incluido el desayuno? – Is breakfast included?

Hága el favor de firmar aquí – Sign here please

Tengo reservada una habitación – I have booked a room

¿Para cuántas noches? – How many nights?

¿Cuál es el precio por día? – What is the charge per day?

Quisiera ver la habitación – I should like to see the room

No me gusta, no tiene vistas – I don't like it, there is no view

Pensión completa – Full board

¿Me enseña su pasaporte? – May I see your passport?

¿Me da otra almohada/manta? – Would you give me another pillow/blanket?

Travelling by plane

For most expats and visitors to Spain, air travel is commonplace and has the advantage of rarely presenting any language problems, though a few may be encountered in Spanish airports, where not all the staff speak English.

Buying something in the duty free shops or taking a drink or a snack in the *cafetería* shouldn't present much of a linguistic challenge, but you might get stuck for words if a customs official takes an interest in your luggage. This seldom happens, though I do remember flying back from a trade fair in London and being asked to open a box I was carrying.

Of course it was carefully tied up with lots of knots and to make matters worse I had no idea what was in it. I explained to the customs officer I was carrying the box for a friend who had already gone through and got a very suspicious look. Fortunately, my colleague came back with a penknife and sliced through the knots. The box contained hundreds of plastic wine glasses for drinking sherry – and an Andalusian flag.

¿Cuántos son? – How many are you?

¿Me enseña su pasaporte? – Would you show me your passport?

¿Tiene Ud. algo que declarar? – Do you have anything to declare?

Abra la maleta – Open your suitcase

¿Tengo que abrir ésta también? – Do I have to open this one as well?

Esto es de uso personal – This for personal use

Es un regalo – It's a gift

¿Puedo cerrar la maleta? – Can I close the case?

Por la puerta número... – Via gate number...

Azafata – Air hostess

Vuelo regular – Scheduled flight

Vuelo charter – Charter flight

Travelling by train

Adverts on Spanish television make much of the comparative safety and comfort of travelling by train, showing passengers enjoying a good meal or relaxing into seats that look far more comfortable than the last one I sat in.

It is true that train services in Spain have improved greatly over the last few years. Some visitors from England recently told me their trip from Malaga to Cordoba was the best train journey they had ever made – and they were amazed that the train left and arrived right on time. In fact, if your train arrives more than five minutes late, you can claim your money back.

Although quite pricey, the high-speed AVE trains that are slowly connecting more and more main cities in Spain are proving fierce competition for domestic airlines, and once the new AVE line to Malaga is complete you will be able to travel to Madrid in just over two hours. Already operating from Malaga is an overnight train that allows you to have dinner, sleep in a bed, take a shower and have breakfast just before arriving in Barcelona. You can take your car along with you, too.

Renfe – *Red Nacional de Ferrocarriles Españoles* – offers a range of incentives, from cheaper fares on certain days to hefty discounts for pensioners. A gold card or *tarjeta de oro* facilitating these discounts can be obtained by pensioners of all nationalities at any railway station by showing their resident's card. The gold card, costing €3, is valid for a year.

Billete para Madrid – A ticket to Madrid

Billete de ida y vuelta – Return ticket

El revisor – Ticket inspector

Mozos de equipaje – Porters

Andén – Platform

Vías principales – Main lines

Primera clase – First class

Segunda clase – Second class

Coche cama – Sleeping car

Asiento reservado – Reserved seat

Coche de fumadores – Smoking carriage

De no fumadores – No-smoking

Furgón de equipaje – Luggage van

Cantina – Station bar

¿Está ocupado este asiento? – Is this seat taken?

Está libre – It's free

¿A qué hora sale el tren para Madrid? – What time does the Madrid train leave?

¿A qué hora llega? – What time does it arrive?

¿Le ayudo a subir la maleta? – Can I help you put your case up?

¿Llega el tren a su hora? – Is the train on time?

¿Hay tiempo para comprar un periódico? – Is there time to buy a newspaper?

¿Tiene parada este tren en Bobadilla? – Does this train stop in Bobadilla?

¿Le importa abrir la ventana? – Do you mind opening the window?

Making reservations

It wasn't so long ago that it was difficult to book anything by phone in Spain. Making reservations for a journey entailed making several trips to the travel agency, and reserving a seat at the theatre or cinema wasn't easy. You had to queue outside the theatre the day before the performance for your ticket, and you went to the cinema on spec. If the film was sold out, you went for a meal instead.

It's true that hotels and restaurants were better geared to taking telephone reservations, but these days you can book just about anything on the phone or internet. The online travel agency run by Ya.com and known as viajar.com reported a 215% increase in bookings during the first months of this year (2004) over the same period the year before.

In Malaga, the newly-opened Picasso Museum reacted to the long queues by advertising a telephone number (901 246 246) for reservations and opened a website (www.unicaja.es) where you can buy tickets. Of course you could spend as much time on the phone as in the queue outside the museum, but at least you can sit down while you wait to get through to the operator.

Quiero reservar una habitación – I'd like to book a room

Con baño, y con el desayuno incluido – With a bathroom, and with breakfast included

La fecha de entrada es el 6, y la salida el 7 – The arrival date is the 6th, and departure the 7th

¿Puedo reserver una mesa para ocho? – Can I book a table for eight?

En zona de no fumadores – In the no-smoking area

Una mesa redonda – A round table

¿Para qué hora? – For what time?

Para las siete y media – For half past seven

Necesito una tarjeta de crédito para confirmar la reserva – I need your credit card details to confirm the reservation

El nombre y la fecha de caducidad – Your name and the expiry date

¿Tiene entradas para la ópera? – Do you have any tickets for the opera?

Prefiero un palco, pero si no, en las butacas – I would prefer a box, but if not, in the stalls

Se han agotado todas las entradas – The tickets are sold out

Para los festivales hay que reservar con mucha antelación – You have to book for festivals well in advance

No quiero hacer cola en la taquilla – I don't want to queue at the box office

No cuelgue por favor, en seguida le atendemos – Please don't hang up, someone will attend to your call soon

Pulse el uno si desea más información – Press "one" for more information

Pulse el dos si quiere hacer una reserva – Press "two" to make a booking

Está en la cola, por favor, no se retire – You are in the queue, please do not hang up

¿En que cine proyectan la película? – Which cinema is the film showing at?

¿Es apta para todos los públicos? – Is it suitable for all the family?

Ya estoy harta de hacer cola, ¿por qué no alquilamos un video? – I am tired of queueing, why don't we rent a video?

IN TROUBLE

I've been robbed!

I have been robbed in Spain, but it was a long time ago and the thief who snatched my purse got away with only 400 pesetas. The other time I was involved in making a *denuncia* to the police was when my parents were mugged by two men while strolling down a quiet path on their way to visit me. They got away with a carrier bag full of dirty clothes and a fan, but one of the thugs knocked down and injured my father while trying to get at his wallet and was only driven off by a well-aimed kick from my mother.

This kind of crime happens more often these days. You hear all the time of people being burgled and having their bags snatched in the street. Before anyone accuses me of scaremongering or – perish the thought! – being negative about life here, let me say that crime in other countries is a lot worse and the south of Spain is still one of the safest places to live.

You might wonder why I bothered to report such a minor incident to the police. There are two very good reasons. Firstly, only reported crimes figure in the official statistics, which can determine how many policemen are employed in your area. Secondly, if you want to claim on your insurance for lost or stolen property, you will almost certainly need your copy of the police report as evidence.

¿Vas a hacer una denuncia? – Are you going to report it to the police?

Quisiera denunciar un robo – I want to report a theft

Bien, ¿me enseña la documentación? – Right, can you show me your identification papers?

No puedo, me la han robado – No I can´t, they've been stolen

Me han robado el pasaporte, el dinero, mis gafas de sol y una cámara – My passport, money, sunglasses and a camera were all stolen

A mi mujer la llevaron a urgencias – My wife was taken to Casualty

Tenía magulladuras y un ataque de nervios – She was bruised and scratched, and was in a state of shock

Ahora está en casa recuperándose – She's at home recovering, now

Ibamos por la calle principal, a la altura de la farmacia – We were walking down the main street, about where the pharmacy is

Se nos acercó un hombre en una moto, por detrás – A man came up behind us, on a motorbike

Agarró el bolso, tirándola al suelo – He grabbed her bag, throwing her to the ground

¿Qué cantidad de dinero llevaba? – How much money did she have on her?

¿Reconocería al ladrón? – Would you recognize the thief?

¿Había más testigos? – Were there any more witnesses?

¿Cómo era? – What was he like?

Alto, moreno, con el pelo largo – Tall, dark, with long hair

Mi madre le dio una patada, donde duele – My mother kicked him where it hurts

Es mejor no luchar – es menos arriesgado – It is better not to fight back... it's less risky

Ya lo sé, pero fue una reacción instintiva – I know, but it was an instinctive reaction

Me dio mucha rabia – I was furious

What to do in an emergency

Don't panic! Keep your head! That's what you are told to do in an emergency, but it's hard to keep calm, especially if you are in a foreign country and you are not fluent in the language. So it's comforting to know that the emergency phone number now in use throughout Europe – 112 – is widely used in Spain, and the operators are trained to take calls in several languages, including English.

So too are the operators of the 902 102 112 number, which can be used to report such incidents as bag snatching or car theft. Not many Spaniards make use of this service, preferring to go along to the nearest police station, but it does save queueing, and gives you 72 hours to go to any police station you choose to sign the report. It works, and in fact if you have forgotten any details in the panic of the moment, these can be added when you go along to sign the report.

Another number worth memorizing is 061, for medical emergencies. The Andalusian Health Service *(SAS)* points out you should call this number only in life-threatening situations such as heart attacks and serious injuries. The medical team will bring an intensive care unit to the patient and give treatment on the spot before making the transfer to hospital.

Los operadores del 112 atienden llamadas en inglés, francés y alemán, además del español – The 112 operators take calls in English, French and German as well as Spanish

El teléfono 112 coordina las emergencias a nivel europeo – The 112 number coordinates emergencies at European level

Movilizan los equipos de emergencia requeridos en un incidente – They mobilize the emergency teams needed for any incident

Contactan con las policías locales, la Policía Nacional y Autonómica, la Guardia Civil y el 061 – They contact the local police, National and Regional Police, Civil Guard and the 061 services

El 061 es el Teléfono de Urgencia Sanitaria de Andalusia para asistir a domicilio a los enfermos – 061 is the Andalusian emergency health service. They send help to the patient

Necesito ayuda, mi marido ha tenido un ataque – I need help, my husband has had an attack

Por favor envíen una ambulancia – Please send an ambulance

Ha habido un accidente – There's been an accident

Está inconsciente, está sangrando – S/he is unconscious, s/he is bleeding

No intente moverla, abríguela – Don't try to move her, keep her warm

La policía va para allá – The police are on their way

El robo del pasaporte no es una emergencia sanitaria – The theft of a passport is not a medical emergency

Debe denunciarlo en la comisaría – You should report it at the police station

Y ponerse en contacto con su consulado – And get in touch with your consulate

"What will they want next? First we have to be nice, then we can't smoke - and now they want us to work!"

R E D   T A P E

Filling forms

If you settle in Spain, it won't be long before you have to fill in a form, either to apply for a permit of some sort, join a club, register your children for school or just send a letter by recorded delivery. Filling in forms is easier than it used to be as more and more of them, especially official forms, come with an English translation.

Even so, confusion can still arise, and the question of surnames is a good example of this. Spaniards have two surnames, the first from the father and the second from the mother, so that the daughter of Juan García Sánchez and Alicia Fernández Pérez, for example, could be called Pilar (or whatever) García Fernández.

Our fictitious Pilar will keep these two surnames for life because Spanish women do not officially take the name of their husband, but when she marries – say to Juan Martínez Blanco – she can if she likes refer to herself as *Señora de* Martínez, which to my mind sounds far less liberated than sticking to the two surnames she was born with.

While on the subject of Spanish names, it's worth mentioning that until a few years ago all Spaniards had to be named after a saint or martyr if they were to be baptised. When this ruling was eventually abolished, there was a crop of children baptised with such names as Constitución and Libertad.

To come back to form filling, some brave foreign residents handle their own paperwork. This is now easy to do with the help of foreigners' departments in town halls and interpreters at police stations, but those who don't want the hassle continue to use the services of the *gestor*, the middleman between you and Spanish bureaucracy, who is happy to sort things out for you, for a fee. You will find him in a *gestoría*, and the fact that this establishment is usually full of Spaniards as well as foreigners will probably reassure you that the fee is worth paying.

Primer apellido – First surname

Segundo apellido – Second surname, (ignore if you only have one)

Nombre – Christian name

Profesión – Profession

Edad – Age

Nacionalidad – Nationality

Lugar de nacimiento – Place of birth

País – Country

Fecha de nacimiento – Date of birth

Sexo – Sex ("H" for *"Hembra"*, female; and "V" for *"Varón"*, Male)

Estado Civil – Marital status

Casado/a – Married

Soltero/a – Single. You can also write *"Divorciado/a"* or *"Separado/a"*

Nombre de padre – Father's Christian name

Nombre de madre – Mother's Christian name

Domicilio (en España) – Home address (in Spain)

D.N.I. (Documento Nacional de Identidad) – Spanish National Identity Card number. (If you are a foreign resident in Spain, write in your *N.I.E (Número de identificación de extranjero)*

Titular – Bearer or holder of any official document

Your town hall

Much of the official business you need to do in Spain will involve going to the *ayuntamiento*, the town hall, where you can pay your local taxes and utility bills (if you haven't arranged for your bank to pay them), apply for a building permit or register yourself as an inhabitant of the town so that you can vote in the municipal elections, that is if you are citizen of an EU country.

Towns with a large number of foreign residents have a special office called the foreign residents' department to assist foreigners in several languages. This is where you can take your queries and find out what is going on in town. Besides their usual work, the town hall organises cultural and social events, evening classes, summer camps for children and regular trips for pensioners, and a lot more.

Consistorio/Ayuntamiento (almost interchangeable) – Town, town council

Trámites municipales – Municipal procedures

Es importante empadronarse – It's important to be on the town census

(Mayor) "Secretary, tell the civil servants I am sorry but there is a powerful reason why I have to freeze their salaries. I have just raised my own."

El Ayuntamiento recibe fondos según el número de habitantes registrados – The Town Hall gets funds according to the number of registered inhabitants

Un pleno consistorial – A council meeting

El Concejal de Cultura/de Urbanismo – The Councillor for Culture/Town Planning

Atención al público – Information/customer services

Coja número y espere su turno – Take a number and wait for your turn

Get ready to vote

It has been some time now since EU citizens in Spain have been able to vote in municipal elections, but so far the number of foreigners who have voted has been disappointing, which is a pity. There are enough foreigners living in Spain now to make their presence felt in the local corridors of power. A few of them have even been elected to office.

It's quite easy to register to vote. All you have to do is go along to your town hall and get your name in the *padrón*, the census list, and obtain a *certificado de empadronamiento* proving you have registered. Once you are on the list, if you are a citizen of the European Union you will be asked if you also want to vote.

Even if you don't want to exercise your right to vote, there is still a good reason to have your name in the *padrón*. The number of officially registered residents determines the amount of Government funds a municipality gets, so the more of us who stand up to be counted, the more funds will be available to provide better local services.

Inscribirse en el padrón municipal – To register as a resident on the municipal census

¿Quiere ejercer su derecho a voto en las elecciones municipales? – Do you want to exercise your right to vote in the local elections?

Acudir a las urnas – Go to the polls

Tener el derecho a votar – To have the right to vote

El electorado/el partido político/el concejal – The electorate/the political party/the councillor

El concejal/la concejala de Urbanismo – The Town Planning councillor

El alcalde/la alcaldesa – The mayor

El Partido Popular, los socialistas, los Verdes – The PP (conservative party), the socialists, the Greens

PSOE (Partido Socialista Obrero Español) – PSOE (Spanish Socialist Workers Party)

El colegio electoral – The polling station

La campaña electoral termina el viernes – The election campaign finishes on Friday

Sábado es el día de reflexión – Saturday is a day of reflection

La abstención suele ser alta – The abstention rate is usually high

Una política de derechas – A right wing policy

Los valores de la izquierda – Left wing values

Simpatizante del centro-derecha – A centre-right voter

Los partidos intentan atraer el voto de los extranjeros – The parties try to attract the foreign vote

"Let he who is free of sin cast the first brick"...
"That just shows how high the cost of housing is."

RELIGION IN SPAIN

Roman Catholic Church

The last three weddings I have attended all took place in packed churches, which got me thinking about religion in Spain. Are Spaniards as religious as they used to be? A Madrid newspaper recently published statistics showing that although just more than 80% of the population say they are Roman Catholics, almost 50% "rarely" go to church and only 18% are regular church-goers.

Perhaps it's no surprise that there are more practising Catholics among the older generation. One example of the flagging interest in religion amongst young Spaniards is the TV quiz game in which a team of three students successfully identified the name of a city at the mouth of the Mississippi and the name of a dog sent into space by the former USSR, but couldn't put a name to the forty days leading up to Easter.)

The statistics specifically excluded attendance at church for baptisms, weddings and funerals, which are considered to be social rather than religious events. The vast majority of Spaniards are still baptized into the Catholic faith, prompting the newspaper to comment: *"España es todavía una nación de bautizados, pero cada año es menos una nación de católicos"* – Spain is still a nation of baptized people, but every year it is less a nation of Catholics.

What puzzles me is that I often read in the newspapers that more and more couples are opting for civil ceremonies or opting out of marriage altogether, and yet the three couples I saw joined in holy matrimony were on a waiting list for months before they could get married in church. Also, I have seen a number of new churches open in my city, Malaga, over the past twenty years, and none have closed. Sometimes the statistics just don't seem to add up.

España es un estado laico – Spain is a secular state

Es aconfesional – It is non-denominational

Los fieles deben mantener la parroquia – The faithful have to maintain the parish

Cuaresma, Pascua, Semana Santa, Navidad – Lent, Easter, Holy Week, Christmas

Hay que confesarse antes de comulgar – You have to go to confession before taking communion

¿Te casas por lo civil, o por la iglesia? – Are you having a church wedding or a civil wedding?

El dieciocho por ciento de los católicos asiste a misa casi todos los domingos – Eighteen per cent of Catholics go to Mass nearly every Sunday

Muy pocos españoles se declaran ateos – Very few Spaniards say they are atheists

Pero hay muchos agnósticos – But there are a lot of agnostics

Es católico/católica practicante – S/he is a practising Catholic

La jerarquía católica – The Catholic hierarchy

A mayor nivel educativo, mayor número de arreligiosos – The higher the level of education, the greater the number of non-religious people

Estos días ya no hay ni Inquisición ni gente que quiere quemar las iglesias – There is no Inquisition these days – Nor people who want to burn down the churches

Semana Santa

The beauty and emotion of *Semana Santa* in Spain are world renowned, and anybody who is lucky enough to be here at this very special time of year should make a point of seeing at least some of the celebrations, which take different forms depending on the region. In the north, passion plays are popular, whereas in the south the events of Easter Week revolve around the religious processions.

Even the tiniest villages take on a new look and atmosphere at Easter, when the holy images are brought out from the churches and carried on floats around the streets, accompanied by brass bands and groups of hooded "nazarenes" and penitents, many of whom follow the long route barefoot and some carry heavy crosses.

The biggest and most famous processions take place in Seville and Malaga. In Malaga, from Palm Sunday to Easter Sunday, the images, borne aloft on gorgeously decorated floats, are paraded through the crowded streets, each one carried on the shoulders of some 130 bearers. The heaviest images are carried by as many as 200 bearers. In the past, these bearers, often brawny dockers, were paid by the brotherhoods, but it is now more usual for young men to pay for the privilege of carrying the floats, which is no light task as it can take them as long as five hours to cover the route.

A word of warning, if you go to the processions on Palm Sunday. Remember to wear something new, otherwise your

"I don't care if it stands for Kyrie, Kyrie, Kyrie Eleison. I am not having it."

hands might drop off. According to an old Spanish saying: *"El Domingo de Ramos, quien no estrena se le caen las manos"*.

Holy Week – Semana Santa

La Virgen – The Virgen

La Procesión – The Procession

Cofradía – Brotherhood

Nazarenos y penitentes – Nazarenes and penitents

Trono – Float bearing the image

Salida del trono – Moment when the float leaves the church

Encierro del trono – Moment when it is returned after the procession

Saeta – Prayer sung to the image

Capirote – Pointed hood

Vela – Candle

Mayordomo – The steward who directs operations

Traslado – Transfer of the image to its starting point – a mini procession in itself

Esta noche sale el Cautivo – Tonight is the procession of Jesus taken captive

Van miles de penitentes detrás – Thousands of penitents walk behind it

Algunos van descalzos o con los ojos tapados – Some of them go barefoot or blindfolded

El trono es portado por más de doscientos hombres – The float is carried by more than 200 men

La Pollinica es el preferido de los niños – The Pollinica (Jesus on a donkey entering Jerusalem) is the children's favourite

Sale el Domingo de Ramos – It takes place on Palm Sunday

En Domingo de Ramos, el que no estrena se le caen las manos – On Palm Sunday you must wear something new (or your hands will fall off)

Las autoridades ven los desfiles procesionales desde la tribuna – The authorities watch the processions from the main stand

Yo prefiero verlos desde la tribuna de los pobres – I prefer to watch it from the poor people's stand (a flight of steps by the river)

Los momentos más emocionantes son la salida y el encierro – The most emotional moments are when the image comes out of the church and is taken back in

El obispo da el primer toque de campana – The bishop rings the bell to start the procession

Este año por primera vez una mujer lleva un trono con los hombres – This year for the first time a woman is carrying one of the images with the men

Sale con el Cristo de Mena – She is in the *Cristo de Mena* procession (Mena was the sculptor of this particular image of Christ)

El Rico ha liberado a un preso – *El Rico* (another image of Christ) has set free a prisoner

Las cofradías, las imágenes, los devotos – The brotherhoods, images, devout followers

El pregón, el traslado, el desfile – The inaugural speech, the transfer of the images (to their starting point), the procession

Of saints and saints' days

One of the pleasures of living in Spain is the extraordinary number of public *fiestas*. And if the holiday falls on a Tuesday or Thursday, it's the custom to make a *Puente*, a bridge, and skip work altogether from Saturday to Wednesday or from Thursday to Sunday. After all, what's the point of going to work just for one day, when the whole family could spend a long weekend on the beach or in the mountains?

Religion plays an intrinsic part in most Spanish *fiestas*, many of which are to celebrate a particular saint's day. Some are observed all over Spain, such as All Saints' Day, when it's customary to go to the cemetery and place flowers on the family grave or niche. Others are local affairs. All towns and villages have patron saints, whose days are celebrated locally with religious services and processions and of course the annual *feria*.

145

Spaniards still celebrate their *santo*, saint's day, rather than their birthday, though it's not uncommon for the two to coincide, when you are named after the saint on whose feast day you are born. Children now tend to celebrate their birthday as well as their saint's day. They sing a Spanish version of "Happy Birthday to You" on birthdays and a song invoking God's blessings, peace and happiness on saints' days.

Santo/Santa – Saint

San – Apocopated form of *Santo*, used before most masculine names

San Valentín – St. Valentine

Día de todos los Santos – All Saints' Day

Los Santos Inocentes – The Holy Innocents

Hoy es mi santo – Today is my name day

Mañana es mi cumpleaños – Tomorrow is my birthday

¡Felicidades! – Best wishes, many happy returns, congratulations, etc.

Feliz Cumpleaños/ Felicidades – Happy Birthday

Feliz, feliz en tu día, amiguito que Dios te bendiga, que reine la paz en tu día, y que cumplas muchos más – Happy, happy on your day, little friend may God bless you, may peace reign on your day, and many (happy) returns

Prayers and the imperative

Christmas always reminds me of the time I married into a Spanish Roman Catholic family and my in-laws, who had heard terrible tales about infidels, including Protestants, were surprised to hear that in England there were also people who celebrated the birth of Christ and that the creed murmured in English churches at Christmas was almost identical to the *credo* in Catholic churches.

"And god bless mummy and daddy, my new daddy, my other daddy's girlfriend, daddy's girlfriend's husband..."

That's some time ago and now Spain of course tolerates and even welcomes other religions, not to mention a small percentage of atheists. Some things just stick in the mind, though, like the devout teacher of Spanish who made us learn the imperative by repeating the Lord's Prayer a hundred times. So here it is, with the imperatives (the formal ones take the form of the verb in the subjunctive – *"sea"*, *"venga"* and *"hágase"*) underlined – for use in church or purely for linguistic practice.

Padre Nuestro, que estás en los Cielos, – Our Father who art in heaven

Santificado <u>sea</u> Tu Nombre, – hallowed be thy name

<u>Venga</u> a nosotros Tu Reino, – Thy kingdom come (to us)

<u>Hágase</u> Tu Voluntad, – Thy will be done

así en la tierra como en el Cielo. – On earth as it is in heaven

Él pan nuestro de cada día <u>danoslo</u> hoy, – Give us this day our daily bread

y <u>perdona</u> nuestras deudas, – And forgive us our trespasses (our debts)

así como nosotros perdonamos a nuestros deudores, – As we forgive those who trespass against us (our debtors)

y no nos <u>dejes</u> caer en la tentación, – And lead us not into temptation (let us not fall)

mas <u>libranos</u> del mal. Amén. – but deliver us from evil. Amen.

"I just get these fits of nervous giggles
at the beginning of the month
when I get what's left of my pension."

FEELINGS

When everything goes wrong

Everybody has days – or weeks – when nothing seems to go right, and it is useful to be able to let off steam or have a good whinge in the right language so that everybody around knows just how fed up or annoyed you are. And it is a fact, is it not, that often the first words you learn in a new language are the ones your grandmother wouldn't have wanted you to hear at all? It must be because expletives are usually short and forceful, so they stick in the mind, or else because you associate them with powerful feelings.

In fact, nobody needs this book to spell out the commoner

swear words in the Spanish language. You only have to listen to a Spaniard speaking to pick them out. Any short words expressed in anger, and which sound as if they should have an exclamation mark after them, are worth remembering for when you next drop the iron on your foot.

But be careful. The Spanish are not generally mealy-mouthed and you could easily end up using words you wouldn't dream of uttering in English. Translations are deceptive anyway, and words that might sound shocking in English are used all the time in Spanish without turning a grandmother's hair. Other expressions, such as the scatological one involving the deity, are fairly common but sound extremely blasphemous to the foreign ear.

Tienes mala cara, ¿Qué te pasa? – You look upset. What's the matter?

Todo me ha salido mal hoy – Everything's gone wrong today

Estoy harta – I am fed up

Estoy muy cabreada – I am very cross

Estoy enfadado/a – I am angry

Estoy furioso/furiosa – I am furious

La gente que me rodea son unos inútiles – Everyone else around me is useless

Todo lo tengo que hacer yo – I have to do everything myself

Estoy hasta el gorro – I am up to here with it

Estoy hasta la coronilla – I am sick and tired

Estoy que echo humo – I am fuming (throwing out smoke)

No puedo más – I can't take any more

Cuando no es una cosa, es otra – When it's not one thing it's another

¡Qué cabreo tengo encima! – I am so cross!

Parece que tienes mala uva hoy – You look to be in a bad mood today

Si, estoy de muy mal humor – Yes, I'm in a very bad temper

Me da ganas de gritar – It makes me want to shout

Bueno, pero no digas tacos – Well, but don't swear

No te pongas así – Don't be like that

¡Vete a hacer puñetas! – Get lost!

How to be sad

Expressing sadness in Spanish is harder than showing you are annoyed or angry. Stamping and waving your arms about can help to let off steam, but there doesn't seem to be an equivalent for being disappointed – not that the Spaniards need to express such emotions all that often, being a fundamentally happy and optimistic set of people.

A World Health Organisation report giving statistics on suicide rates in different countries had Spain way down at the bottom of the list, along with the UK, Mexico and Jordan. Lithuania and Russia were way up at the top. Apparently, the belief that Swedes are prone to suicide is a myth. Closer to home, it's thought Tarifa has the highest suicide rate in Spain because of the constant wind that drives the locals to extremes, but I haven't been able to find statistics on that one.

Estoy muy triste – I am very sad

Tiene los ánimos por el suelo – His/her spirits are at rock bottom

Sufre una gran depresión – He/she is suffering badly from depression

Pareces deprimido. ¿Qué te pasa? – You look depressed, what's the matter?

Estoy depre – I am depressed (colloquial)

Te estás ahogando en un vaso de agua – You're making a mountain out of a molehill (drowning in a glass of water)

El clima aquí me deprime – The weather here depresses me

Lo veo todo muy negro – Everything looks black

Está de capa caida – He/she is down in the dumps

¡Qué pena! – What a pity

"Now they've finished the motorway
I wonder what excuse Manolo will come up with
for getting home late every night."

O D D S   A N D   E N D S

The *Mañana* Syndrome

The 19th century essayist Mariano José de Larra had a lot to say about the *Mañana* Syndrome. He wrote a whole short story about it, which many of us can still relate to, having met the characters in countless banks, government offices, and other places we have been to, thinking we could sort out our business in half an hour and be back at work before anybody noticed we'd gone.

The hero, or rather victim, in Larra's story is a foreigner in Madrid named monsieur Sans-delai, who arrives in Spain with letters introducing himself to the writer and outlines his plans for the following week – three days to establish his genealogy and prove his identity to the authorities, one day to put forward his business propositions, which will either be accepted or rejected, and three days of sightseeing.

Six months later he is tired of being told to come back tomorrow, and goes home. The following is an excerpt:

"Vuelva usted mañana," nos respondió la criada, "porque el señor no se ha levantado todavía" –
"Come back tomorrow," the maid told us, "because el señor isn't up yet."

"Vuelva usted mañana," nos dijo al siguiente día, "porque el amo acaba de salir" –
"Come back tomorrow," she told us the next day, "because the master has just gone out."

"Vuelva usted mañana," nos respondió al otro, "porque el amo está durmiendo la siesta." –
"Come back tomorrow," she replied the day after, "because the master is sleeping the siesta."

"Vuelva usted mañana," nos respondió el lunes siguiente, "porque hoy ha ido a los toros" –
"Come back tomorrow," she replied the following Monday, "because today he has gone to the bullfight".

¿Qué día y a qué hora se ve a un español? Por fin le vimos. "Vuelva usted mañana," nos dijo, "porque se me ha olvidado la cita. Vuelva usted mañana, porque no está en limpio" –
On which day and at what time can one see a Spaniard? We finally saw him. "Come back tomorrow," he said, "because I had forgotten our appointment and the final draft isn't ready yet."

Sounds somewhat familiar? When dealing with official-dom, it's wise to take along with you as many documents as you think you may need, and more, and also have photocopies ready, just in case. And leave plenty of time for the meeting.

The other alternative is to employ a gestor to do the legwork for you. For a reasonable fee, the *gestor*, to be found in a *gestoría* will know what documents have to be submitted and which office he needs to, queue in on your behalf.

Trámite – Procedure

Lo tenemos en trámite – the papers are in, it's being dealt with

Oficina de atención al público – Public information office

Está tomando café – He/she is having coffee

Está desayunando – He/she is having breakfast

Está reunido/a – He/she is in a meeting

Ha salido un momentito – He/she has just popped out for a second

Cartas de recomendación – Letters of recommendation

Tiene que traer su partida de nacimiento – You have to bring your birth certificate

Traducida al español – Translated into Spanish

Por un traductor jurado – By an official (sworn) translator

Necesita tres fotos tamaño carnet – You need three photos, identity card size.

Tengo un buen enchufe – I have a good contact (literally, a plug)

Conozco personalmente al jefe – I know the boss personally

Voluntary work and charities

Everyone feels generous around Christmas, which it why at this festive time a huge number of charity events are held. And everyone, it seems, has their favourite charity. In general, foreigners living in southern Spain have the reputation of being particularly keen supporters of animal charities, while Spaniards are quick to give one-off donations for disaster relief in any part of the world.

They are also active and hugely successful in raising funds for underprivileged children, and will contribute readily to requests for funds from charities run by religious orders or to any appeal connected to Latin America, presumably because of family and historical ties.

The favourite charity with many expats on the Costa del Sol is Cudeca, a worthy international organisation founded by an English woman that cares for terminal cancer patients. It has the distinction of being truly international, serving both the Spanish and foreign community.

Una asociación benéfica – A charity

Recaudan fondos para una buena causa – They raise funds for a good cause

Operación kilo – Operation kilo (in which shoppers buy an extra kilo of food for a charity)

Para el Tercer Mundo, para los niños – For the Third World, for children

Para un orfanato – For an orphanage

Para los pobres – For the poor

Para los sin techo – For the homeless

Para los ancianos – For the elderly

Para los animales abandonados – For abandoned animals

Muchos españoles compran los "Christmas" de Unicef – Many Spaniards buy Unicef Christmas cards

Un concierto benéfico – A benefit concert

Donar fondos – To donate funds

Día Internacional del Voluntario – International Volunteer Day

Organizar una rifa – To organize a raffle

Los voluntarios son personas altruistas – Volunteers are altruistic

Trabajan para ayudar a los menos afortunados – They work to help the less fortunate

Cudeca atiende a enfermos de cáncer – Cudeca looks after cancer patients

Y tiene un centro de cuidados paliativos – And has a palliative care centre

Telling the time

It may be a cliché, but in southern Spain time seems to move more slowly than elsewhere. Having had plenty of time – years, in fact – to think about it, I have come to the conclusion that it is because time seems to stop in the middle of the day for an hour or two, and continues for longer in the evening.

After the midday break, the day starts all over again, so that whereas in northern climes there is only time in the evening for a meal, a bit of TV and maybe a short visit to the pub, the Andalusian evening has time enough for another stint at work, a gathering with friends for *tapas*, maybe a football match on the telly, a leisurely dinner with the family and a last drink or two before bed. It's like having two days in one.

Unpunctuality could be another factor that slows down the time here. A five o'clock appointment in the afternoon could mean any time between five and six and when you are invited to a party or dinner at nine o'clock, you are not expected to turn up until 9.30.

The mornings are just as elastic. Although technically they end at midday, por la mañana is more likely to mean any time before lunch, which is around three o'clock.

¿Qué hora es? – What time is it?

Perdón, ¿tiene hora? – Excuse me, do you have the time?

Son las nueve – It is 9 o'clock

Es la una de la tarde – It is 1 pm

Son las dos y cuarto – It is quarter past two

Son las tres y diez – It is ten past three

Las cuatro y veinte – Twenty past four

A las nueve menos cuarto – At a quarter to nine

Son ya las siete menos veinte – It is twenty to seven

Llegamos tarde – we'll be late

La película empieza a las siete menos cuarto – The film starts at a quarter to seven

Vemos las noticias de las diez – We watch the 10 o'clock news

A medianoche salen las brujas – The witches come out at midnight

Al mediodía hace demasiado calor para estar al sol – At midday it is too hot to be in the sun

Nos vemos debajo del reloj a las cuatro y media – We'll meet under the clock at half past four

Mi reloj está adelantado – My watch is fast

El tuyo está retrasado – Yours is slow

El reloj de pared/el reloj de pie – The wall clock/ the grandfather clock

El reloj de la cocina marca las cinco – The kitchen clock says it's five o'clock

Me levanto a las seis de la madrugada – I get up at six in the morning

Madrugas mucho. Yo suelo trasnochar – You get up very early. I tend to stay up late (all night)

Por la mañana trabajo – I work in the morning

Por la tarde quedo con mis amigos – In the afternoon I meet my friend

Por la noche ceno con la familia – In the evening (late) I have dinner with the family

Domingo/lunes/martes/miércoles – Sunday/ Monday/ Tuesday/Wednesday

jueves/viernes/sábado - Thursday/Friday/Saturday

Los jóvenes salen el viernes por la noche – Young people go out on Friday night

Regresan a casa cuando sale el sol – They return home when the sun comes up

Only one bookshop

Our local daily newspaper has commented more than once on Malaga's reputation for having hundreds of bars but only one bookshop. I have not personally counted the bars in the city to confirm this claim but most people seem to be of the opinion that *Malagueños* are fonder of bar-hopping than they are of reading books.

They are not alone, it seems. Research shows that Madrid is said to have much the same proportion of taverns to bookshops, about 40 per cent of all Spaniards never, or almost never, read a book. Newspapers fare better, but not by much, in least not in Andalusia, where about 30 per cent read one every day, as opposed to more than 60 per cent in Navarra.

This is all rather surprising when you consider the increasing number of campaigns the educational and cultural authorities are launching to encourage people to read more, the regular book fairs, temporary libraries installed on the beaches in summer, and the racks of low-priced books in the bigger supermarkets.

However many bookshops Malaga might have, perhaps they should follow the trend taking hold in other countries and serve coffee on the premises, though one suspects if would take something a little stronger than coffee to persuade people to come in and browse.

Más de cien tabernas y una sola librería – More than 100 taverns and just one bookshop

Hay una buena librería de segunda mano aquí – There is a good secondhand bookshop here

Una novela histórica – An historical novel

Una novela romántica/policial – A romantic/detective novel

Literatura infantil – Children's books

Ficción/una biografía/una autobiografía – Fiction/a biography/an autobiography

Un diccionario/una enciclopedia – A dictionary/an encyclopedia

Un libro de arte/de historia/de ciencia – An art/history/science book

Un libro de texto – A text book

Harry Potter ha vendido un millón de ejemplares – Harry Potter has sold a million copies

¿Tiene un libro de cocina española? – Have you got a Spanish cookery book?

No leo casi nunca – I hardly ever read

Leo todos los periódicos todos los días – I read all the newspapers every day

Prefiero las revistas de moda – I prefer fashion magazines

La prensa amarilla – The tabloid (yellow) press

Muchos jóvenes estudian en la biblioteca – Many young people study in the library

Los libros son muy caros – Books are very expensive

Hay más de una librería en Malaga – There is more than one bookshop in Malaga

Existen por lo menos dos – There are at least two

"Come on Raul...we can't go home
without your father. Where did you bury him?"

Proverbs and sayings – 1

Researching Spanish proverbs and sayings for an article, I was
struck by how many are related to religion. Spain, of course,
although officially a secular state, is still largely Roman
Catholic – and to judge by the number of new churches being
built, religion is not even on the decline in this country.

In fact, a church has been built quite recently in a tourist
resort on the Huelva coast, paid for by regular holidaymakers
and owners of second homes in the area, which reminded me
of the one I saw this summer in Brighton, England, which
had been converted into a business centre.

Oddly enough, their religion does not seem to prevent
Spaniards from taking the lord's name in vain in daily
conversation, sometimes in a very blasphemous manner.
Neither do they give a second thought to invoking God on
any and every occasion, whether they be believers or not.

Estar en el séptimo cielo – To be in seventh heaven

Vive como un cura – He lives like a king (a priest)

Dios aprieta, pero no ahoga – God tempers the wind to the shorn lamb.

Hacerlo como dios manda – Do it correctly (the way God ordains)

A quien madruga Dios le ayuda – God helps those who help themselves

¡Vaya por Dios! – Good lord!

¡Cielo santo! – Good heavens!

Nunca digas de este agua no beberé – There but for the grace of God go I (never say I won't drink this water).

El infierno está lleno de buenos propósitos – The road to hell is paved with good intentions

Cuando el diablo no tiene qué hacer, con el rabo mata moscas – The devil finds work for idle hands (when the devil has nothing to do, he kills flies with his tail)

El hábito no hace al monje – Clothes do not make the man (the habit doesn't make the monk)

Más vale malo conocido que bueno por conocer – Better the devil you know

Dios mediante – God willing

El hombre propone, y Dios dispone – Man proposes, God disposes

Dios no quiera – Heaven forbid

Dios te bendiga – God bless you

Proverbs and sayings – 2

Many of the other stocks phrases and sayings in Spain are

very much like their equivalents in English, but the differences can also be striking. For example, where English speakers know that hatters are the epitome of craziness, in Spain the goats are as mad as hatters.

And while Spaniards are invariably tickled pink by the idea of pet animals raining down on us in a storm, it is really not so amusing to have "pitchers full of water" being dumped by the clouds. Animals figure largely in both Spanish and English sayings, with a few variations in the species.

Está como una cabra – He/she is as mad as a hatter (*cabra* – goat)

En menos que canta un gallo – In the shake of a lamb's tail (*gallo* – cockerel)

La carne de burro no es transparente – You are blocking my view (*burro* - donkey)

Más vale pájaro en mano – A bird in the hand is worth two in the bush (*pájaro* – bird)

Está lloviendo a cántaros – It is pouring down (by the pitcherful)

A donde fueres, haz lo que vieres – When in Rome, do as the Romans do

Cada maestrillo tiene su librillo – We all have our own way of doing things

Aprobé por los pelos – I passed by the skin of my teeth

Antes de que te cases, mira lo que haces - Look before you leap (before you get married)

De tal palo tal astilla – A chip off the old block

En casa del herrero, cuchillo de palo – Shoe-makers' wives go barefoot

Voy a hacer lo que nadie puede hacer por mí – I am going to spend a penny

Más vale tarde que nunca – Better late than never

Díme con quien andas y te diré quien eres – A man is known by the company he keeps

Es más listo que el hambre – He/she is as sharp as tack

No tiene pelos en la lengua – He/she doesn't mince words

No andes por las ramas – Don't beat about the bush

Estoy ciego, borracho como una cuba – I am blind drunk, drunk as a skunk

Me importa un pepino – I don't care a hoot

Por mi madre que no he sido yo – I swear it wasn't me

Todo va viento en popa – Everything's going smoothly

Amigos or *Amig@s*

In the area of sexist language, Spain is still lagging behind most other European countries but some progress has been made. Spaniards will now often write *amig@s* instead of *amigos y amigas* and they will use terms such as *el/la propietario/a*, rather than assume the owner has to be male.

In the professions, too, words such as *médica* and *abogada* are creeping into usage, no doubt to the delight of all female doctors and lawyers. There is still a problem, though, with marital status. Should a woman be addressed as *señora* or *señorita*? And should she have to state whether or not she is married, when men get away with being called *señor*, whether they are married or not?

Worse than being asked if one is married, however, is the question *¿Señora de...?* This request for your husband's name is best met with a glare and a statement of one's own name. Glaring at official documents doesn't, in my experience, have much effect on them, but you can always cross out *"don"* and *"el interesado"* and write *"doña"* and *"la interesada"*.

And when letters continue to arrive from your bank addressed only to the male holder of your joint account, complain to the manager. If that doesn't do it, change your bank.

Se utiliza "señora" para mujeres casadas – You use *"señora"* for married women

La palabra "señorita" se usa para solteras – The word *"señorita"* is used for spinsters

Existe un manual andaluz sobre lenguaje no sexista – There is an Andalusian manual of non-sexist language

Es para administrativos/as – It is for administrative personnel

Opta por un mayor uso de los colectivos – It recommends greater use of collective nouns

Se puede usar "la dirección" en vez de el/la director/a – You can use "the management" instead of the director

Una bombera – a firewoman

Una concejala – a female councillor

Una jueza – a female judge

Una arquitecta – a female architect

Todas son palabras bastante nuevas – All are fairly new words

Las mujeres siguen siendo discriminadas – Women still suffer from discrimination

Y son peor pagadas – and they are more poorly paid

Es una lucha constante por la igualdad – It is a constant struggle for equality

Superlative descriptions

As soon as you get fairly to grips with the Spanish language, you will almost certainly get involved in an interminable discussion with someone about the relative richness and variety of the two languages – yours and theirs. For some reason it is a matter of pride to Spaniards that Spanish often has three or four words for the same thing, while English speakers will delight in catching out Spanish friends with the weird pronunciation and spelling of English words.

I remember a Spaniard once telling me that "good, better, best" just stands no chance against the resounding *"bueno, mejor, buenísimo"*. Yes, I knew the equivalent was really *"bueno, mejor, el mejor"* but I agreed with him that it doesn't have the same ring to it.

The *"ísimo"* suffix makes a word superlative, though, and you can put it at the end of most adjectives if you want to sound very enthusiastic or just exaggerate your case. *"Estoy cansada"* (I am tired) sounds quite tame, but tell everyone you are *"cansadísima"* and you stand more chance of getting some sympathy.

If that doesn't work and you are asked to fetch something which is *"lejos"* (far away) or *"lejísimo"* (a very long way away), you can always refuse on the grounds that it is *"en el quinto pino"* (at the fifth pine tree or the back of beyond).

Likewise, there superlatives for describing good things. A meal can be *"bueno"* (good), *"buenísimo"* (extremely good) or *"de puta madre"* (not for use in very polite company as the literal translation has to do with prostitutes and mothers, but among friends it would mean "absolutely delicious").

Mi madre es buena cocinera – My mother is a good cook

Mi abuela es mejor cocinera que mi madre – My grandmother is a better cook than my mother

Mi hermano es el mejor cocinero del mundo – My brother is the best cook in the world

Cocina mejor que nadie – He cooks better than anyone

Hace unos postres buenísimos – He makes wonderful desserts

Y unas ensaladas riquísimas – And absolutely delicious salads

Mi hermanita es tan alta como yo – My little sister is as tall as I am

Es altísima para la edad que tiene – She is very tall for her age

Pero es menos inteligente que su prima – But she is less intelligent than her cousin

Su prima es inteligentísima – Her cousin is extremely intelligent

Yo soy fuerte, pero tu eres más fuerte que yo – I am strong, but you are stronger than me

Eres tan fuerte como Goliat – You're as strong as Goliath

Pero menos fuerte que David – But not as strong as David

David era muy fuerte – David was very strong

Y le gustaba el café fortísimo – And he liked extremely strong coffee

Eres muy simpático – You are very nice

Eres simpatiquísimo – You are extremely nice

¡Qué amable eres! – How kind you are!

Eres realmente muy amable – You are really extremely kind

Favourite words

Does everyone have favourite words and expressions? I don't mean the sort the Spanish call *"muletillas"* or crutches, which you fall back on when you are stuck for a word. Rather, I refer to the words that always make you smile or the phrases you like but I can't seem to translate.

Often it is the literal translation that is apt and makes you smile. An example that comes to mind is a *"salto de cama"*, which translates as négligée, but when you think that *"salto"* is a jump and *"cama"* is a bed, and in Malaga it is also called a *"tontito"*, something small and silly – well, that is the sort of expression I mean.

Be warned, though. If you hear a word and like it and decide to add it to your vocabulary, first make sure it is acceptable in polite company. I once said quite innocently to a very upright citizen *"Es un cachondeo."* I thought I was saying it was a bit of a lark, but the expression at the time suggested the beginning of an orgy. *"Eres muy cachondo"* can still mean you are either a real laugh or randy.

No me siento muy católica hoy – I don't feel very well (very catholic) today

Te he visto mirarle el canalillo – I saw you looking down her cleavage (little canal)

Eres un chaquetero – You're a turncoat (jacket swapper)

Siempre hacen de mí la cabeza de turco – They always make a scapegoat of me (a Turk's head)

Cabeza de chorlito – Bird brain (head of a little plover)

Enaguas – Petticoat, underskirt (in waters)

Nos pegamos una tarde de miedo – We spent a wonderful afternoon (*de miedo*, of fright, is often used in Spain to indicate something very pleasurable.)

Calavera – Skull

Panaché – A mixed vegetable dish (sometimes prepared without much panache)

¡Jesús! – Bless you! (after a sneeze)

Echarse flores encima – To sing one's own praises (throw flowers over oneself)

Este mes andamos apretados – Money is a bit tight with us this month

Aguafiestas – A party pooper, wet blanket, spoilsport (water-party)

Es un sieso – He's an asshole (perhaps slightly less vulgar in Spanish)

La hostia – Host (religious sense of the word)

Hostiar – To belt someone

Te voy a dar una hostia – I'm going to give you a good beating

Se pegó una hostia con el coche – He had a really bad car crash

Un picadero – A riding school or exercise ring. Also a bachelor pad

Last word

I would like to end this book with the first full sentence my parents learned in Spanish. When they came to visit, they liked to speak Spanish when they went shopping. They loved Spain but were not so keen on some of the inhabitants that invaded their home. They still remember how to say:

¿Tiene algo para matar las hormigas? – Have you got anything to kill the ants?

For a free catalogue of all our books
on Spain contact:

SANTANA BOOKS
Apartado 422,
29640 Fuengirola (Malaga).
Phone 952 485 838.
Fax 952 485 367.
Email: sales@santanabooks.com
www.santanabooks.com

UK Representatives
Aldington Books Ltd.,
Unit 3(b) Frith Business Centre,
Frith Road, Aldington,
Ashford, Kent TN25 7HJ.
Tel: 01233 720 123. Fax: 01233 721 272
E-mail: sales@aldingtonbooks.co.uk
www.aldingtonbooks.co.uk